THE other AMERICA

Teen DROPOUTS

These and other titles are included in *The Other America* series:

THEotherAMERICA

Teen DROPOUTS

by
Gail B. Stewart

Photographs by
Carl Franzén

Lucent Books, P.O. Box 289011, San Diego, CA 92198-9011

Cover design: Carl Franzén

Library of Congress Cataloging-in-Publication Data
Stewart, Gail 1949–
    Teen dropouts / by Gail B. Stewart; photographer Carl Franzén.
      p. cm. — (The other America)
    Includes bibliographical references and index.
    Summary: Uses four case studies of teenagers who dropped out of high
school to explain who drops out and why and to examine the economic
and social consequences of such a decision.
    ISBN 1-56006-399-8 (lib. bdg. : alk. paper)
    1. High school dropouts—United States—Juvenile literature.
[1. Dropouts.]   I. Title. II. Series: Stewart, Gail, 1949–   Other America.
LC146.6.S74   1999
373.12′913′0973—dc21   98–27051
                                                 CIP
                                               AC

Printed in the U.S.A.
Copyright © 1999 by Lucent Books, Inc.
P.O. Box 289011, San Diego, CA 92198-9011

Contents

Foreword

O, YES,
I SAY IT PLAIN,
AMERICA NEVER WAS AMERICA TO ME.
AND YET I SWEAR THIS OATH—
AMERICA WILL BE!
    LANGSTON HUGHES

Perhaps more than any other nation in the world, the United States represents an ideal to many people. The ideal of equality—of opportunity, of legal rights, of protection against discrimination and oppression. To a certain extent, this image has proven accurate. But beneath this ideal lies a less idealistic fact—many segments of our society do not feel included in this vision of America.

They are the outsiders—the homeless, the elderly, people with AIDS, teenage mothers, gang members, prisoners, and countless others. When politicians and the media discuss society's ills, the members of these groups are defined as what's wrong with America; they are the people who need fixing, who need help, or increasingly, who need to take more responsibility. And as these people become society's fix-it problem, they lose all identity as individuals and become part of an anonymous group. In the media and in our minds these groups are identified by condition—a disease, crime, morality, poverty. Their condition becomes their identity, and once this occurs, in the eyes of society, they lose their humanity.

The Other America series reveals the members of these groups as individuals. Through in-depth interviews, each person tells his or her unique story. At times these stories are painful, revealing individuals who are struggling to maintain their integrity, their humanity, their lives, in the face of fear, loss, and economic and spiritual hardship. At other times, their tales are exasperating, demonstrating a litany of poor choices, shortsighted thinking, and self-gratification. Nevertheless, their identities remain distinct, their personalities diverse.

As we listen to the people of *The Other America* series describe their experiences, they cease to be stereotypically defined and become tangible, individual. In the process, we may begin to understand more profoundly and think more critically about society's problems. When politicians debate, for example, whether the homeless problem is due to a poor economy or lack of initiative, it will help to read the words of the homeless. Perhaps then we can see the issue more clearly. The family who finds itself temporarily homeless because it has always been one paycheck from poverty is not the same as the mother of six who has been chronically chemically dependent. These people's circumstances are not all of one kind, and perhaps we, after all, are not so very different from them. Before we can act to solve the problems of the Other America, we must be willing to look down their path, to see their faces. And perhaps in doing so, we may find a piece of ourselves as well.

Introduction

THE FACTS ABOUT TEEN DROPOUTS

"I've never liked school," admits sixteen-year-old Will. "I don't read fast enough, and I have trouble with understanding what I read. I can do math, but I never seemed to do good on the tests. School was stressful; I always felt nervous walking into a classroom.

"When I turned sixteen, I was so glad. My mom said I had to stay in until sixteen, because that's the law. But after that, she said I could make my own decision. She wasn't happy I was dropping out, but she knew I hated going. And the way I figured it, I'd rather be spending my days working than sitting in class, just getting D's and F's. So when my birthday came around—boom! I was out the door!"

Will is far from being the only member of his high school class who dropped out before graduating. In his suburban Milwaukee school, a full 25 percent of the students who begin as freshman do not graduate for one reason or another. Experts say that a 25-percent dropout rate is better than average—the national rate is about 32 percent. However, they point out, in some urban schools in New York, Chicago, Los Angeles, and Detroit, the rate can be as high as 60 percent of the total school population.

"Nationally, about a million kids each year leave school before graduating," one Minneapolis counselor says. "And that's a million too many. We know about it, but we aren't doing enough to prevent it. It's a source of national shame."

A HIGH PRICE TO PAY

Teens who choose to drop out of school before graduating pay a high price in the job market. According to 1993 figures, the employment rate for boys who don't graduate is only 67 percent of the rate for boys who receive their high school diplomas. Girls who drop out have an employment rate of only 59 percent of the rate for girls who graduate.

Many of the dropouts who do become employed find themselves in dead-end jobs, working in fast food, janitorial, or data entry positions. Such jobs usually pay very little; they are considered "dead-end" because no matter how efficient a worker becomes, there is no hope of promotion. Callie, who quit school at age seventeen to work at a fast food chain in a Chicago suburb, says that it took five months for her to realize how boring her job was.

"It was fun at first," she says. "I liked having the noon to six shift because I could sleep late—lots later than getting up for school at 6:30 every morning! And the job had different things about it—learning the different machines, the cash register, the fryer. But after awhile it was just repeating itself, every day. I couldn't see myself doing that job every day. I can see what they mean about dead-end jobs now, 'cause I got one."

TRAPPED

Many of the disadvantages faced by dropouts cannot always be measured in economic terms, although they may start with a lack of money. For example, young people who don't finish school are seldom prepared to compete in society. Losing interest in the few options for employment that are open to them, they are more likely to suffer from a lack of self-esteem. As a result, they are also more likely to become criminals or to engage in substance abuse. A 1995 Department of Corrections survey, for instance, found that almost 80 percent of inmates in American prisons are high school dropouts.

"Of course, not every dropout is a criminal or a drug user," says counselor Debra Thorson. "But being trapped in a life of poor jobs with no hope of growth is not an ego-builder. People can cope with temporary hardships, such as when a young person works two jobs to put himself through college, for instance. The paycheck doesn't stretch to allow a movie or dinner out, and that can be difficult—but we know it isn't going to be like that forever. On the other hand, the dropout often falls into a *life* of such hardships, and because of her lack of education, cannot get out of it. And that starts the cycle of low self-esteem and despair."

EVERYBODY PAYS

It is not just the teen dropout who pays the price of leaving school too early. The lack of education costs American businesses over $25 billion each year in on-the-job education for workers who lack some of the most basic skills in reading, writing, and math. Many business owners say that many of the young people applying for jobs cannot read manuals or add fractions to compute hours for billing.

"We're not talking advanced calculus here," says one plumbing supplier. "But a guy who has trouble with what I consider pretty basic math just can't do justice to the job. It costs me time and money correcting his mistakes later on."

Dropouts cost the taxpayer, too. Statistics say that teens who drop out of school are far more likely to require welfare benefits than those who stay in school. In 1992 high school dropouts were three times as likely as high school graduates to receive money from Aid to Families with Dependent Children (AFDC), food stamps, or other public assistance programs.

It's Not Like It Used to Be

Many teens who consider dropping out of high school point to their parents or grandparents who did the same thing years ago.

"My grandpa left school when he was fourteen," says a Minneapolis teen. "He got a job with a construction company, and he did real good—even ended up being a foreman. He could support a family of four on his salary."

Years ago it was much easier for young people to earn a living without a formal education. They might join the army and learn a skill that way or choose from an array of skilled jobs that (back then) did not require a diploma, such as auto mechanic, plumber, or carpenter.

That isn't the case today, however. Most skilled positions are learned in trade or technical schools, which require either a high school diploma or its equivalent. Today's armed forces, too, require a diploma.

Times have changed, too, for girls who drop out of school. In times past, a girl might have reasoned that she would be a housewife and mother—neither of which would require a complete high school education—and her husband would financially support the family. Today, however, soaring divorce rates have resulted in many women having to find jobs to support themselves and their children. And even if a marriage stays intact, rising costs often make two incomes necessary to raise a family.

Who Drops Out?

In 1988 the National Center for Education Statistics (NCES) did a study of students in grades eight through twelve. In addition, NCES conducted follow-up studies in both 1990 and 1992. The center found that at least one-fourth of the girls who drop out of high school do so because they are pregnant. The figure is somewhat higher among African Americans (34 percent) and Hispanics (31 percent). Although schools do not require pregnant teens to leave school, many say attending school is very difficult.

"I was pregnant while I was a freshman in high school," says Gladys, now nineteen. "If it was up to me, I'd have left right away. But the counselor got me to stay at least till I was about five months along. I hated it; I felt sick and couldn't stand sitting there learning stuff that had nothing to do with me."

Another teen mother, Shelley, recalls how difficult it was to get up early for school when she was pregnant. "I was always sick in the mornings," she says, "and I was always tired. It was hard paying attention, especially in the early part of the day. When I dropped out, I figured I'd go back after the baby was born. But it didn't work out that way, so I started working at Taco Bell. I wish now I'd gone back and gotten that diploma."

Many teen counselors report that although there are options for teen mothers to return to school—including programs that offer free or reduced-cost day care—few young mothers return.

"We find that about three-fourths don't return," says one high school counselor. "They find they are so busy taking care of the baby—and often working a part-time job to support themselves—that they have neither the energy or the inclination to sit down and do the necessary homework to pass high school classes."

Many Other Reasons

Some teens drop out of school because family problems become so intense that school is a low priority. Sometimes divorce causes so much friction within the home that teens cannot concentrate on schoolwork. Occasionally teens run away from home because they are physically, sexually, or emotionally abused.

"I left home because my father was hitting me all the time," says Gerald. "I tried just staying out of his way at first, but that didn't always work. So when I was in tenth grade, I ran. I stayed away eight months and ended up missing so much school I just quit for good."

Gang violence is another reason teens drop out of school. Some are participants in gangs and find that gang activity is more exciting than school. Others stay away from school because they fear gangs and the violence they cause. In 1994, 7 percent of students aged ten to eighteen reported being threatened or injured with a weapon on school property, and over 16 percent were in a physical fight at school.

Teens who drink or use drugs are high risks for becoming dropouts, too. Almost all schools have a policy of suspending or expelling students who use or sell drugs or alcohol in school; during such suspensions, young people can get further and further behind in their studies.

Alice, one of the young people interviewed for this book, received help for her substance abuse problems but later dropped out of school. She felt it was dangerous for her to be in school socializing with the same people who had supported her drug and alcohol abuse. "I worried that I was putting myself in risky behavior," she explains, "and that was just asking for trouble."

LEARNING PROBLEMS

By far, though, the most common reason for teens leaving school before graduation is poor performance. For a variety of reasons, when students fail or consistently have difficulty doing schoolwork, they lose interest. As one sixteen-year-old remarked, "Why should I sit in a room day after day proving how stupid I am? Even if the teacher doesn't say it, the other kids see me getting big red F's on my tests. Who needs it?"

In a great many cases, it is not a question of students being slow or incapable of learning. In an estimated 60 to 75 percent of cases, a teen has a learning disability that makes it difficult for her or him to learn through the more traditional methods used by teachers. Some have a disorder that interferes with their ability to sit still and concentrate; others have problems such as dyslexia, which is a disturbance in their ability to read and do math.

Educators estimate that between 4 and 5 million school-age children in the United States have learning disabilities. "We know now that millions of children in the past have been mislabeled as 'slow' or 'underachievers' when that hasn't been the case at all," says one reading specialist. "Children who were constantly scolded for not paying attention, or criticized for doing sloppy work, or ridiculed by their peers for being unable to read from their readers, usually left school for good as fast as the state would allow it."

Another special-education teacher agrees. "Teachers used to think these kids weren't smart. Now we know different—most of them are very bright. A learning disability has only to do with *how* someone learns, not whether he or she *can* learn." Experts say that as clinical specialists become more proficient in diagnosing learning problems, teachers can vary the methods they use to accommodate such students.

A MORE SPECIFIC LOOK

The four teens whose interviews appear in this book have varied reasons to explain why they dropped out of high school. LeAnn, fifteen, left school the day she gave birth to her daughter. Even before, her school experiences had not been positive, she says, because of social problems between herself and another group of girls. She says she would consider returning to school but is not sure when that will be. Her days are spent visiting friends and watching television.

Alice, seventeen, is a former substance abuser who missed a great deal of school during the past few years. She left school because she worried that the strides she made in becoming sober would be lost by returning to an environment where alcohol and drug use are widespread.

David, eighteen, became involved with an Asian gang when he entered junior high. As he ascended higher and higher in the gang, he found school unappealing. "I didn't have time for it anymore," he says. Instead, his days were filled with drive-by shootings, selling drugs, and hanging around with his friends in the gang.

Matt, eighteen, has also had unpleasant experiences in school. When his parents transferred him to a prestigious college-prep school in the suburbs, Matt felt out of place. As a city kid from a racially mixed neighborhood, he was ridiculed and snubbed by his classmates. Although Matt is clearly bright and articulate, he has had difficulty in school, especially with reading. (His teachers suspected a learning disability, but he was not diagnosed.) Matt dropped out early in his senior year but hopes to enter a technical school.

Some of the stories contained here are a sad commentary on the state of education in America. The descriptions of students drinking alcohol in coffee mugs, gang fights, and teachers being driven

13

from their classrooms by unruly students are disturbing. It is clear that schools have failed in many cases. But also included in these stories are the teens' admissions of laziness, poor decision-making, and dishonesty with their parents.

In each of their stories, the four teens expressed regret that things have not worked out; however, they all exhibit some hope that their education is not over. Whether they graduate by taking an equivalency exam or enroll in an alternative school, there remains the real possibility that they can improve their current situations.

LeAnn

"IF I *DID* GO BACK, I'D DO BETTER.
I'D CONCENTRATE MORE ON THE
WORK, DO MY HOMEWORK. I
THINK I'D USE MY TIME BETTER
BECAUSE THERE ISN'T AS MUCH
OF IT AS THERE WAS BEFORE I
HAD THE BABY."

Author's Note: LeAnn, fifteen, dropped out of school for the same reason as many girls her age—she became pregnant. Now living at home with her infant daughter, her life consists of watching talk shows on television and occasionally visiting friends. She seems puzzled why anyone would question her decision to keep and raise her baby herself—even though she has little hope of getting any kind of satisfying employment. She does mention the idea of finishing high school, but she is unsure at this point. The paperwork involved with getting county-provided day care and transportation seems overwhelming to her.

The house is small and square, nestled in a quiet section of the city's north side. LeAnn answers the door; she is cradling a tiny baby in her left arm. She looks more like a young teenage babysitter than a mother. She has to change the baby's diaper, she explains, so she motions for me to wait in the living room.

The room is small and tidy, with a long sofa and armchairs. A large family portrait hangs on one wall, a framed print of an eagle on another. The room is dominated by a large television, which is tuned to a daytime talk show, booming at full volume. The program features several young women yelling at one another, arguing about a young man named Richard. They all feel that they should have a claim on him; Richard is laughing and clapping as he watches one woman stand up and pull another's hair.

After a few minutes LeAnn returns with her baby, whose name she says is Lanayaiah. It's easy to see that LeAnn is shy—almost painfully so—and has trouble making eye contact. Motioning me to an overstuffed chair, she sits on the sofa and busies herself with the baby, unnecessarily smoothing the baby's hair and fussing with the sleeve of the green-and-white sleeper. The baby is drowsy, but she jumps with a start as the noise level of the television increases.

"I'M NOT DECIDED YET"

LeAnn turns the sound of the program down—somewhat reluctantly, for she then has no reason to look away at the television. She takes a deep breath and begins to speak.

"I dropped out of school seven weeks ago. Actually it was seven weeks and three days—I know that real well because that's exactly how old Lanayaiah is. She was born on the last day I was in school," she says with a trace of a smile. "Yeah, I went to school right up to when the baby was born. So if I go back, I'd still be a freshman in high school because I didn't finish that year."

She emphasizes the word *if*. Does that mean that she might choose *not* to return to school?

"I'm not decided yet," she shrugs. "There's things about school that I like, but there's a lot that I don't like. I'm just not sure right now what I'm going to be doing."

She looks down at Lanayaiah and strokes her cheek, stealing a look at the muted television.

"I WAS ALWAYS SORT OF SHY"

Even though she is ambivalent about school now, LeAnn maintains that her early school experiences were positive.

"I looked forward to going to kindergarten," she says. "I remember having new school shoes that I had to wait to wear. I wanted to put them on the day I got them, but my mom made me wait until the first day.

"We used to live downtown—in fact, we've only lived here on the north side for about a year. This isn't bad, but downtown was terrible. It was so loud, and the crime was scary, too. My mom and dad didn't take us kids outside too much; there wasn't anyplace to really play, you know?

LeAnn poses with her infant daughter, Lanayaiah. After giving birth during her freshman year, LeAnn dropped out to care for her baby.

"So kindergarten sounded fun. We got to play games and go outside for recess and do lots of coloring and singing and things like that. I was always sort of shy back then, so I had a little trouble talking to the teachers. But with kids my own age it was okay."

LeAnn smiles. "I'm better now, I think. I'm still pretty shy around people I don't know, but I'm not scared of them or anything. I just am pretty quiet."

THE VALUE OF EDUCATION

LeAnn's parents were interested in her starting school, she says, partly because she is the oldest child in her family and it was a new experience.

"They were excited for me," she remembers. "My parents knew how important an education was. They both had an education. See, my dad is from West Africa, from Liberia. He came to the United States when he was a teenager, I think. There was a war going on over there, and it was really dangerous. Lots of innocent people were getting killed by the army—people in his own family.

"He wanted to have a good future, so he came to this country, even though he really didn't have much. He lived in Detroit for a while, and then he came here. He went to college up north, graduated with a science major. But the bad part is that because of the differences between our schools and the ones in Liberia, some of the classes he took over there didn't count here.

"He works in a nursing home right now—not the job he wanted. He says that if we all lived in Liberia, he'd have a good job and be making lots of money. But here, it's not that way. And he sure doesn't want to move back to Liberia because it's just as dangerous now as it was then.

"Anyway, he has plans to go back to school. He's going to get his master's degree, so he'll be doing better. He does pretty good in school; he's good at understanding things like that."

Her mother, she says, did not go to college.

"But she finished high school," she says. "She's not Liberian, no. She's Native American—Chippewa. And she's got a pretty good job right now. She works at a factory not too far from here, doing soldering."

"EIGHTH GRADE WAS A NIGHTMARE YEAR"

School went pretty well until her eighth grade year, says LeAnn. She wasn't always the best student, but she usually did her work and didn't cause trouble in class.

"I know sometimes I was lazy," she smiles. "I sometimes didn't do the homework; or, if I did it, there were times I just went through it real fast or I turned it in late. But usually the teachers were nice enough, and they let me have a little more time to finish it.

"But eighth grade, that was the worst. Eighth grade was a nightmare year for me. I was going to this one school, Sanford. And there were a bunch of girls there that I was having trouble with. They hadn't been there the year before, no. So they didn't even know me, but we started having some problems."

When asked what sort of problems, LeAnn shrugs.

18

"See, these girls were black. And they started making lots of comments in the hall about me, about my hair. See, it's long."

She reaches up and fingers a long ponytail swept on top of her head.

"Those girls, they had short hair, and they didn't like my hair. But see, I'm half Native American, so I have different hair than them. I know it sounds really stupid, but the comments really got

LeAnn says that both of her parents highly value education and were eager for her to start school. Despite her parents' support, LeAnn became discouraged during her eighth-grade year, when fellow students started harassing her.

to me. They'd laugh and call me names and stuff like that; they'd say things that would hurt my feelings, and they didn't care. They just stood around in this group, about ten of them, and talked about other people really loud, anybody who's different than them. Just picking on people, you know?

"I guess I got to where I didn't want to stand it anymore. One time at school I yelled back at one of the girls, and the principal gave me and her a one day suspension."

THE FIGHT

LeAnn says she only had a couple of friends that year. And, she says bitterly, she ended up fighting one of them.

"Yeah, fighting," she says with a rueful smile. "Real fighting, with punching. See, it started like this: I was friends with Shauna and Billette. We all three were friends, but something happened.

"See, Shauna had written me a note in school. She told me some things about Billette, some things she didn't like. It wasn't really any big deal. I had the note in my room, and one time Billette came over to my house and saw it. She was just hanging around and it was right there, so she read it. I didn't even know she'd seen it; I sure wouldn't have shown it to her.

"So Shauna found out about Billette reading that note, and she was so mad! She accused me of showing it to Billette on purpose, to split them up as friends or something. She figured she was going to get excluded or something, I guess."

LeAnn shakes her head in disgust.

"I never would have done that. I don't stir up trouble like that— that's more like something those girls at school would have done, but not me. Anyway, Shauna wouldn't let it alone. She came up to me in the hall, really mad. She comes right up and starts calling me mean names, telling me how bad a friend I was. And she hits me, with a closed hand, right in the face! Right in the middle of school!"

How did she respond? LeAnn looks a little embarrassed.

"I hit her back," she admits. "I didn't want to because she's real small, way smaller than me. But I couldn't take that—her calling me those names and just punching me with everybody standing around looking."

REPERCUSSIONS

LeAnn remembers that as soon as she punched Shauna, two teachers materialized out of nowhere.

"One grabbed her and the other one grabbed me," she says. "They took us both aside and asked us what was going on, why we were fighting like that. We went down to the principal's office and we each had to tell our side of the story.

"Well, as it turned out, I got suspended—again! This time it was for five days. Shauna only had a three-day suspension. And it was really hard telling my father this time. He'd sort of understood about my getting into trouble yelling at that one girl, but this time he was mad. He said, 'God, LeAnn, you've got to stop getting into trouble with these girls at this school. We've got to get you out of here before any more trouble starts!' And my mom, she was the same way. They weren't happy with me at all about that."

LeAnn says that the worst part of the suspension wasn't being out of school for a week, it was thinking about coming back.

"I was just dreading it," she says, shifting Lanayaiah to her other arm. "It was all I thought about. I'm telling you, I was getting sick to my stomach thinking about walking back in there and seeing all those girls, and this time Shauna would be with them, instead of me!"

"MY MOM . . . EVEN STARTED CRYING"

"And I was right, too. My mom brought me to school when my suspension was up, and we walked in the front door together. Those girls were just waiting for me. They were so mean, they walked right up to us and started hassling me in front of my mom. They were putting their fingers practically in my face, laughing.

"My mom was really amazed at how bad they really were," she says. "She got really angry with them—so upset and angry that she even started crying. She came into the principal's office and started telling the principal about how I shouldn't have to be treated this way—our family shouldn't be treated this way. She told him that those girls had even been calling my house, fooling around on the phone, saying stuff and hanging up. It wasn't right that things like this should be going on, and the principal agreed.

"But there was really nothing he could do—at least that's what we were told. He assigned a hall monitor to escort me to my classes so they wouldn't keep hassling me. I guess I needed protection, but it made me feel weird—I hated that."

Nothing Left to Do

Were the boys at her school as unfriendly as the girls? LeAnn shakes her head.

"No, they weren't as bad," she says. "Usually they could be sort of nice. I mean, there were a couple of them that went along, that laughed when those girls started saying things; but most were okay.

"And here's the funny thing about those girls," she adds, remembering something. "It was kind of strange. When they were together they would harass me, call me names, whatever; but

LeAnn was relieved to start her freshman year at a new school, away from the bullies she had encountered during eighth grade. Although she didn't realize it at the time, ninth grade would be LeAnn's final year of school.

when they are on their own, like they see me on the street or something, they start talking to me! They act like I'm their friend or something! That seemed so crazy to me; I didn't want nothing to do with them, even when they were trying to be nice. And I *did* try a couple of times to talk to them, to ask them why they were like that. But I got nowhere, so I just let it alone."

LeAnn says that things weren't as bad once she got into her classroom.

"The teachers were pretty nice most of the time," she admits. "I know they knew about what was going on—they felt sorry for me, I could tell. They'd talk to me, saying, 'Hey, LeAnn, just ignore those girls. Don't you get into trouble on account of them—they aren't worth it.'

"But as time went on and things didn't improve, they agreed that I'd be better off at a different school. This was in the spring of eighth grade. They talked to my mom about it, urged her to apply to get me transferred out of there."

LEAVING SANFORD

LeAnn's parents agreed that it would be best for her to leave Sanford and transfer to another school; however, she says, such a transfer was not something that happened quickly.

"This was in the spring," she says. "And I was waiting a whole month at home before the paperwork and everything could get done. The principal at my old school had to wait until things could get figured out, and a new school would have space for me. I don't know why it had to take so long, but it did. And by the time I got started at the new school, there were only a couple weeks left before summer vacation!"

The transfer was basically useless since LeAnn entered high school in the fall. As it turned out, her ninth grade year was her final year of school.

"I never thought about it being my last year," LeAnn says quietly. "I figured I'd keep going to school, especially now that I was in high school—a different one than those stupid girls in eighth grade! They all went to another school, so I wasn't about to have problems with them any more. Now, I guess, they're hassling someone else—they're somebody else's problem.

"High school started out okay for me. I tried to be friendly to pretty much everybody. I didn't get real close to anyone, either—

just stay to myself and not make enemies, you know? See, the thing with those other girls is they spend a lot of time talking and talking about what so-and-so said, and who she said it to, and what it all meant. It's just gossip, and they like to spread it around. Lots of times it wasn't even true—just exaggeration of something I said, but they took it wrong. It's better just to stay private, I think."

A New Relationship

There were some things in LeAnn's life during her freshman year that she particularly wanted to stay private—among them a new boyfriend.

"His name is Carl," she says, displaying little emotion. "He's the father of my baby. I met him the spring of my eighth grade year, around my neighborhood. I was with some friends and just walking around, you know, on a nice day. He was hanging around, too; he has relatives that live in my neighborhood.

"He's a good-looking boy, yeah. He's dark-skinned, tall, kind of thin. He has real pretty eyes—that's one thing I noticed about him right away," she admits. "He was older than me—I was 14 and he was 18. Anyway, we got to talking, and we started going out."

"Going out" was a sexual relationship, LeAnn explains, and says that Carl was not her first. The two would go to his aunt's house when no one was home.

"We didn't use birth control, no," she says wearily. "He didn't; I didn't. It wasn't that I felt like I'd be lucky and not get pregnant. I guess I wasn't even thinking about anything like that, not even thinking at all. And a while later I found out that, yeah, I was pregnant.

"I'd missed my periods, you know, and felt kind of tired. Plus, my stomach felt—I don't know—sort of hard, I guess. Not like normal. I went to the clinic and had a test done there. The doctor told me I was pregnant, that there was no doubt."

LeAnn says she thought briefly about having an abortion because she knew her parents would be angry with her for getting pregnant.

"But I just couldn't. The more I thought about it," she says, "it seemed wrong. And I knew that adoption wasn't the answer. I couldn't ever carry a baby and then just turn it over to somebody else to have. So the only thing I *could* do was keep it, so I did."

24

"I Was Scared"

Telling her parents was something LeAnn was not prepared to do. She confided only in her friend Darshae, and hoped that Darshae could keep her secret as long as possible.

"I was scared, you know," she says, sighing. "I didn't want anybody to know because they'd give me lectures, tell me what to do, tell me how stupid I was to get pregnant when I was so young. I didn't want to hear any of that, not from anybody.

LeAnn and Lanayaiah wait at a bus stop near their home. When LeAnn discovered she was pregnant at age fourteen, she says she was too scared to tell her parents. She was able to conceal her pregnancy until she finally went into labor.

"It was real hard being pregnant, especially at first. I'd get up and feel so sick, and I'd just feel like going back to sleep. But I had to get up and go to school—get on that smelly old bus. If I didn't, my parents would wonder what's going on, and I didn't want them suspicious. So I just kept quiet about it. And at school it was hard, too. I felt sick to my stomach, especially during first hour. And sometimes I'd just put my head down on my books."

Even as the months went by and her stomach started to swell, LeAnn kept her pregnancy a secret.

"I wore a lot of big shirts," she smiles. "That and baggy pants with elastic at the waist. But even then it wasn't easy to fool people. My parents asked me over and over again if I was pregnant—I think they had been suspecting something like that—but I denied it. My dad would come right out and say, 'LeAnn, are you pregnant?' and I'd get mad and say, 'No, are you?'"

LeAnn giggles. "He still reminds me about that, even now."

LYING AT SCHOOL

As surprising as it may seem, LeAnn was able to conceal her pregnancy at school—even as her due date approached!

"I'll tell you one thing," she says firmly. "It was really hard in gym. My stomach was big under that baggy shirt, and when we had to lie on the floor and do pushups, I didn't think I'd make it. And when we'd play basketball or something like that, I'd be a little nervous that someone would get rough and bump into my stomach. I was real protective of myself that way.

"I hadn't told anyone except Darshae, and I didn't intend to. So if I thought that whatever we were doing in gym would be too hard to do, or dangerous or something, I'd just sit out. There are plenty of girls who do that, for lots of reasons.

"When I was about eight months along, some of the kids at school were questioning me, just like my parents were. This one boy was watching how I was walking—you know how pregnant girls kind of waddle side to side? Well, he finally said—real loud— 'Hey, LeAnn! You *pregnant* or something?' And I told him, 'No, I'm just fat!' I don't know that all those people would have been critical of me, but I just wasn't ready to tell.

"But one of my teachers, Miss Bell, finally found out. I didn't tell her, but she intercepted a note my friend and I were sending back and forth during math class. You know how sometimes a teacher will see you passing a note and she'll just come over and take it

26

and maybe read it over? Well, she did that. And after class, Miss Bell talked to me. She told me I should go see the social worker at the school, just so they knew about my condition."

"IT WAS JUST EASIER TO LIE"

What about Carl? Did she keep her pregnancy from him as well? LeAnn shrugs.

"He found out eventually from one of my friends. I'd been lying to him, just like I'd been lying to my parents. After he found out, I saw him at the store; he was like, 'So LeAnn, you're pregnant, huh?' I'm like, 'Yeah.' I didn't expect him to be too involved. I mean, it's not like we were going to get married or anything.

"So things just went on; I kept getting bigger and bigger. I went to school right up to the day I delivered. That day I had no idea that I was going to deliver later on—it just seemed like any other day. I got home and at about 7:00 I started feeling like maybe something was happening. My water broke around 10:00 and then it started for real! I was lucky because the whole thing was really short. I've heard that first babies sometimes take a while, a long time. But Lanayaiah was born just before midnight.

"I remember my mom coming to the hospital. She was mad at me and very hurt. She told me then about how disappointed and mad she was about the way I handled the whole thing. She said, 'How come you never told us?' I felt bad, I really did. I mean, I always had a pretty good relationship with her. We talked about things, usually.

"I don't know why I didn't tell her. I just knew they'd be disappointed in me and mad. My mom and dad—they both expected more of me, and I knew that. So it was just easier to lie than face that. So that's what I told her.

"She told me that she wasn't angry at the baby. It wasn't Lanayaiah's fault. It was hard for her to accept this baby, but she'd do it. And she did—both her and my dad. They didn't know Carl very well and had no idea that we'd been having a relationship. They blamed me more for lying, for not doing the right thing and coming to them right away. But they accepted the baby; it took a while for it to happen, but it happened."

"I'M PRETTY DULL"

Lanayaiah, who has been sleeping in LeAnn's arms, becomes wakeful now. She squirms and begins whining, trying to find a more comfortable position.

Since dropping out of school, LeAnn says that her days are quite mundane—mainly spent at home watching TV while looking after her baby.

"My life now isn't very exciting," she says. "In some ways, I miss school—being with kids my own age. But during the day it's just me and her since my mom and dad go to work in the morning. I watch television, read the paper. Really, that's about it. I don't feel tied down with the baby, I guess, because I've never really been the type to be gone from home a lot.

"If I felt like going out later in the day, I could. I've got brothers and sisters—two brothers, fourteen and eleven, and two sisters, thirteen and six—and they like to come home from school and play with the baby. But even though they are more than willing to take her from me, I usually hang around here, too. Maybe at some point I'll want to get a job or something at night, but that's a ways off. I mean, Lanayaiah's not even two months old yet.

"Sometimes if I do go out, I go shopping. That's one thing that's fun; if I have any money at all, I like shopping for her. It's fun to buy her a cute outfit or some shoes, or even some diapers or something. She's growing already—it's easy to see how fast she'll grow out of all this newborn stuff she's wearing now."

LeAnn smiles at the baby, who is hiccuping noisily.

"But as far as like going out to movies or stuff like that, no. I don't really like going out to eat or stuff like that. It sounds like I'm pretty dull, but that's me."

FINISHED WITH SCHOOL?

Although she has dropped out of school, LeAnn says she is still undecided about whether her future will include education.

"Lately my father has been talking to me a lot about going back to school," she says. "He kind of gives me pep talks, you know, saying that I got good grades one time, so I could again. Finish high school, he says, but I don't know.

"I mean, he's right in one way. I did good in school, mostly before that bad eighth grade year when there wasn't so much bad stuff going on. I liked things then, especially English and math. I got an A in English. Back then I was on the B honor roll and did extra things like student council.

"And I *do* understand about getting an education—why that's important," she adds. "My mom's sister and her kids were staying with us for a while, for about two months. They'd been in a shelter because she was on welfare and couldn't make payments on her apartment. They'd come by here because the food was so bad at the shelter, and my mom would cook for them and stuff.

"In a way that was scary for me, thinking about how that could happen. I mean, my aunt is a good person, not lazy or anything. And I sure wouldn't want to be in a situation like she was in, with Lanayaiah, going around from shelter to shelter. When it's someone you know, someone in your family, you think about that. And it usually isn't the people that have a good education in the shelters, I guess."

LeAnn says that her father tells her that bad things can happen to anyone, but it's best not to rely on luck too much.

"He says that if you've got education, you've got choices," she says. "You can always find a job if you've got a diploma. Even if it isn't the best job right away, at least you can bide your time while you look for a better one, and there'll be food on the table while you're looking."

She sighs, thinking. "I know what he says makes sense."

THE HARD PART

The hardest part about returning to a school situation, LeAnn says, is being so different from everyone else.

"I'd be a mother," she says simply. "Most of them wouldn't be like me at all. I mean, a lot of my friends from school were so surprised when they called me and I'm like, 'You want to see my baby?' I think they thought that when I said 'my baby' I was talking about my boyfriend or something! I mean, it was so strange— they would see me out shopping or something with her in the stroller and they'd say, 'LeAnn, whose baby is that?'

"Some of the teachers would be okay if I went back. You know that one I was telling you about, Miss Bell, the math teacher? Well, she's called me a few times since the baby was born; wants to know how I'm doing. And she even sent over a package with some baby clothes and things. That's pretty nice; not many teachers would do something like that.

"So that gets me thinking about going back sometimes. Not everyday, no," she insists. "Just sometimes. But it would be hard because I'd have to get day care; I've got nobody to watch Lanaya-iah while I'm gone because my parents work. And even though you can apply for free or reduced-cost day care through the county, it takes a while to get it started."

LeAnn smiles sadly. "The classes probably would not be the hardest part, really. It would be wondering what the other kids at school would be like. If I met up with some kids like those girls in eighth grade, I don't know what I'd do. Probably walk right out the door and never go back! It's just not worth it to me to have problems like that at school. No school would be worth it."

LOOKING AHEAD

Assuming she did return to school at some point, what would she like to do with her life? LeAnn smiles.

"I'd like to do hair—I'm pretty good at it," she says, giving her own long hair a toss. "I'd like to go someplace and learn more about that. Or maybe a lawyer. That looks fun when you see it on TV, but I don't know too much about it. If I decided I *really* liked school, maybe I'd aim for that. But being a stylist would be fun. My dad has a sister who's thinking about opening up a beauty shop. Maybe I could help her out, learn some things while I'm finishing high school, like after 4:00 in the afternoons or something."

What about Carl? LeAnn shrugs.

"He's not really a big part of her life. I see him around sometimes. He's got relatives in Chicago that he goes to visit a lot, so he's gone pretty often. When I see him, I guess we get along okay, but it's not like he's my boyfriend or anything. I don't think I'm interested in having a boyfriend right now. In fact, that's probably the last thing I need. I'm already busy taking care of a little baby.

"I know that eventually I'd like to move away from here. I don't like it too much. I mean, right here where my parents live isn't too bad because it's kind of quiet. But downtown where we used to live? It was terrible—lots of gangs, lots of noise.

"My younger brother was over at Elliot Park—you know where that is? He was just there hanging around with some friends, and some Crips were around there, too. They were shooting at this other gang, and my brother almost got shot right in the face! He's not in any gang, you know, he was just there. But he was leaning against a wall and moved his head—and zing! A bullet hits the wall right where he was standing. He said there were bullets flying everywhere. So that's what I mean. It isn't safe, not for little kids or anyone."

THINKING ABOUT BEING A MOTHER

LeAnn looks down at Lanayaiah, who has fallen asleep again.

"I know I want to keep her safe. I really like just thinking about her, you know? Just like when I'm holding her while she's sleeping, I think about how she's going to talk, what her voice is going to sound like. Or I think about what she's going to look like when she's my age. Her eyes and nose are like me, I know that.

"When she was born, she was a lot lighter-skinned, but she's getting darker now, like Carl. Sometimes I think about her as a teenager. That's really strange to think of her like that, but I do. Sometimes my dad says, 'What are you going to do if she comes home pregnant at fifteen like you? How would you like being a grandmother when you're thirty?' He's kidding, but only partway. I know that it's a big responsibility raising Lanayaiah. I want her

LeAnn proudly holds a sleeping Lanayaiah. "When I'm holding her while she's sleeping," LeAnn says, "I think about how she's going to talk, what her voice is going to sound like."

to like school; I want her to do good when she starts out and not get in any trouble or get pregnant too soon. I'd like to send her to college so she can be anything she wants to be."

"I Learn from My Mistakes"

LeAnn admits that she has a problem with low self-esteem.

"I don't know about me," she says with a sorrowful smile. "Sometimes I'm not too sure if I really like myself or not. I'm in between, I guess. Like, I know I goofed off too much in school before, and I didn't get much done. I wasn't rowdy or anything, I just didn't apply myself, and the good teachers that I had knew it. The bad teachers—well, I don't know what they thought, and I don't really care. Some of them don't even take the time to care about the kids one way or the other.

"I wasn't honest before, either—and that's one thing about last year that I wish I could take back and do over. Especially when my parents were asking me about whether I was pregnant. I never told them the truth and that hurt them, I know.

"My dad is telling me to focus on the future. He gives me lectures, you know? And I get mad, but really, I know he's right a lot of the time. If I think about the future, I think the best thing would be to go back to school sometime. I learn from my mistakes, I think. I'd hang around better people, stop being with people who fool around and make noise in class, stuff like that. See, that's what happened in my science class; that's why I had an F at the beginning. People around me were just talking and talking, and nobody was listening to the teacher.

"I knew that was wrong, even when I was doing it. But you know, it's hard when you're this age, and my parents forget that. So do the teachers. It's so easy for older people to tell you, 'You shouldn't have done that; you should've told me about this.'

"So," she says quietly, "if I *did* go back, I'd do better. I'd concentrate more on the work, do my homework. I think I'd use my time better because there isn't as much of it as there was before I had the baby."

LeAnn sighs softly and shifts in the chair. She lays the sleeping baby on the sofa cushion next to her.

"I really want to set a good example," she murmurs, almost to herself. "I want her to be better than me."

Alice

"I'VE DROPPED OUT OF SCHOOL
BECAUSE OF DRUG AND ALCOHOL
PROBLEMS. A USER—YES,
DEFINITELY; I'VE BEEN A BIG
USER."

Author's Note: Alice, seventeen, dropped out of school during her junior year. A user of drugs and alcohol for years, she has been sober and clean for six months, but upon returning to school, feared that she would slide back into bad habits. Alice's descriptions of abundant drug and alcohol use are unsettling; however, her parents' lack of concern about her drinking is even more so. "They chalked a lot of it up to that 'teenagers will be teenagers' thing," Alice explains. But even though she blames herself for being a good manipulator, one has to wonder if her substance abuse problems would have been as severe had her mother and father taken them more seriously early on.

Alice opens the door and smiles apologetically.

"I'm really sorry," she says. "I got in from work just a minute before you showed up. Come on in and grab a can of pop or something."

She leads the way into a lovely old home on the city's south side. The living room and kitchen are immaculate; the hardwood floors gleaming. There is a definite smell of furniture polish in the air.

She laughs delightedly as she grabs two cans of pop from the refrigerator. "That's because of my mom. She's a total freak about cleanliness—honestly, she can't be home more than two minutes before she starts scrubbing or polishing something. She's always really kept our house looking great."

Alice curls herself into a chair on the porch. She is an attractive seventeen-year-old with light brown hair streaked from the sun. She is tan and lean and could be the poster child for healthy living. Her appearance makes her next statement seem impossible to believe.

"I've dropped out of school because of drug and alcohol problems," she says matter-of-factly. "A user—yes, definitely; I've been a big user."

"My Parents and I Agreed That I Should Leave School"

"If I were in school now, I'd be a junior," she says. "Basically, I ended up going to treatment because of my substance abuse, and I was out of school for three months or so. After that three-month period—what they call the primary-care program—I went back to school.

"But after two weeks I could tell it wasn't going to work out. I just knew I couldn't stay sober and clean if I stayed."

She flashes a grin. "You don't know me, but I'm a real manipulator. I just have a way of doing it to people, of making them do what I want them to do. I figured I was going to manipulate the teachers and counselors into letting me get out of class and get back into the patterns I'd been in before, when I was using.

"I didn't use during that two-week period," she insists, "but I was hanging out with a lot of the same people I'd hung out with when I was drinking and stuff. So my parents and I talked about it. We discussed the options—switching to another public school or maybe enrolling in a private school. But it kind of seemed that no matter where I went I'd probably have the same problems. So my parents and I agreed that I should leave school. For the time being, yeah—I'm a dropout."

Beginnings

Alice pours some Fresca into her glass.

"I guess I should start at the beginning, so all this makes sense. I'm the youngest of two children. My sister, Rose, is five years older than I am. I have a real problem with self-esteem, measuring up to other people's expectations and things like that."

Alice acknowledges that people say she seems very poised, very self-assured.

Alice and her mother sit together on their porch. Alice says that she and her parents ultimately decided that it would be better for her to drop out of school and focus on recovering from her substance addiction.

"A lot of that is because I've always been involved in things—softball, dance, ice skating, basketball—you name it. It seems like I've got lots of confidence. But I don't," she says firmly. "I don't at all. I have a problem with all my imperfections. I mean, the only reason I tried in school or anything else was just so I didn't look stupid to everyone else. The *only* reason. It wasn't for the pleasure or the enjoyment. I saw no value in those things other than their use in getting people to accept me or like me."

"Odd One Out"

Alice says that in order to understand her lack of self-esteem, it's important to understand her family.

"See, I've always felt like the odd one out in our family," Alice continues. "I mean, my mom and dad are incredibly smart and talented. They were *both* valedictorians of their high schools! My dad is a manager or something downtown in the post office; my mom is director of the neighborhood Meals-on-Wheels program. They're very driven, very straight, very conservative.

"My mom and I aren't alike at all. She's always been the best at everything; she was raised in the South, and her father was very strict with her. I joke with her, telling her she's an obsessive-compulsive. If you come to my house after she's been here just a half hour or so, she's got the house spotless. She's always moving around, working, cleaning, making lists."

She laughs. "I'm really a laid-back person, so she really drives me crazy. My dad is less that way, although he's really talented. He's incredibly smart and really talented musically. He writes music, and he's got a great singing voice. He's real active in our church."

Alice sighs. "I'm really proud of him. But even though he can do all those things, he's a little more relaxed—at least in some things. So we're alike in that way. And my sister, Rose—she's right in the middle. Not like me, not like my mom."

Measuring Up

Alice says that Rose was a tough act for a younger sister to follow.

"She did everything in school," Alice says. "She's always had good grades and was in every activity possible. She played softball, tennis, basketball; she was on the high honor roll. And it always seemed so *easy* for her.

"Not for me, though," she says shortly. "I've always been a real procrastinator. No motivation whatsoever. I never did homework—even back in elementary school. I don't like to read. I'd have books to read for a test and then bring them home the night before and try to do everything at the last minute. I just didn't care."

Alice insists that her trouble isn't lack of intelligence.

"I'm as smart as the kids who are getting A's," she says. "I'm a smart person—I test well. I *can* do the work, I just *don't*. I think

I'd be better off doing something that I could learn from experience rather than from a lecture or a book or something. I learn better watching someone do something, I think. But I'm not stupid.

"I always felt that I wasn't good enough when I was small. It always seemed as though if I really wanted to measure up, I'd have to work very, very hard. I think my parents instilled that feeling in me, too—not on purpose or anything, not realizing how stressful it was for me. But they always told me how things weren't impossible because Rose did it. Or other kids they knew could do this and this and this."

Alice motions sharply with her hands in the air and then suddenly drops them.

"So then *I* should be able to do those things, too. They'd say, 'Those girls are getting good grades, Alice, so you can, too.' Or, 'Rose made the high honor roll, so you can, too.' That's the kind of thing that would really stress me out."

"I DREADED IT"

Alice says that she never really enjoyed being at school, even when she was younger.

"I dreaded it," she says with a smile. "I cried and faked being sick a lot. All the time in elementary school, I'd just ask the teacher to send me to the nurse. I remember in first grade, standing down in the cafeteria at lunch, crying. I just wanted to go home, and my teacher wouldn't let me.

"My mom eventually figured out the whole thing. At first, you know, she was sympathetic—I'm sure she really thought I was sick. But after a while she decided not to let me stay home unless I had a fever or was throwing up or something, some outward sign."

Was there any class, any part of school that she enjoyed? Alice frowns at first.

"Well, I hated math, science, and history. They were the absolute worst," she says. "The only part of history that interested me was the Civil War because the whole concept of slavery was so bizarre to me. It's interesting to read about it or learn about the South—how people could rationalize it or fight a war to protect the right to have slaves. It's just so odd. So I enjoyed that stuff, but the rest of it was really pointless as far as I was concerned."

At seventeen, Alice's young life has been extremely complicated. She was kidnapped and molested as a child and suffers from an inferiority complex.

KIDNAPPED

There was one incident during her elementary school years that Alice says affected her in a major way.

"I was kidnapped," she says bluntly. "Our family had gone to Ohio for my uncle's funeral. We were staying in a hotel there, and I was taken from the hotel lobby. I was gone overnight and, yeah, they caught the guy. He was a nineteen-year-old; a stranger.

"The thing was, I was sexually abused by my kidnapper. Not raped, but sexually abused. And I didn't tell anyone. I didn't tell the police, and I didn't tell my parents, not until much, much later. But afterwards I was really afraid of my father. I didn't want to do anything with him or be near him. I totally excluded him from my life. So my parents got me into therapy because they didn't know what to do about that. And I sort of ended up really needing the outlet that therapy provided for me."

"I LIKED THE TASTE"

Alice takes a long swallow of pop, as if to clear her thoughts.

"Anyway, that was part of my childhood. And so was drinking. I think the first time I really got drunk I was in third grade. We'd go up to this cabin every year—it belongs to a friend of our family. They invite us up, along with six other families. There was lots of stuff going on, lots of fun.

"I figured out how to sneak drinks from my parents and the other adults there. Not to show off for the other kids, no! It was because I liked the taste. That's unusual for a kid, I think. It was mostly hard liquor, like gin and tonics. See, in our family it's always been okay to have a sip of Dad's beer or a little taste of the wine at Thanksgiving. So I'd take advantage—being a manipulator even then!

"I'd come up to my mom and say, 'Oh, can I have a taste of this?' And she'd say, 'Okay, but just a little bit.' And then I'd guzzle it and laugh and act silly, joking around, you know? She'd tell me it wasn't funny. But then later, when she wasn't looking, I'd go and grab it and walk away. It's amazing how adults just don't even notice things. She'd look around eventually and wonder where it was, but then she'd just figure she'd misplaced it or something and go make another one.

"I remember being really tired, just so sleepy. And I only say this because it is the first memory I have of how good alcohol tastes. It has always tasted good to me, always."

LOTS OF PARTIES

Alice says she became "a drinker" when her sister was in high school and had parties—parties she herself attended.

"I was younger than they were, sure," she shrugs with a smile. "But it wasn't a problem. My parents were gone—they'd sometimes go on these weekend marriage encounters, you know? And Rose would have kids over and there'd be some drinking going on. And I was right there.

"When Rose went away to college in Madison, Wisconsin, our family would go down to visit her. My parents had friends in Chicago who had a son that went to the same school, so the grown-ups would get together. I'd go off with my sister's friends and hit the bars or go to parties. And I looked pretty much like I do now when I was 13, so I didn't get carded."

Alice dismisses the idea that her parents were permissive.

"They didn't really understand," she says. "I know occasionally, they'd know there had been some drinking, just like they knew Rose had parties. But they figured some of this stuff was just normal teenager stuff, you know? Nothing bad happened, so it wasn't a big issue. I'm sure if they had known the extent of it all they'd have put a stop to it. But I was a good liar."

STARTING ON DRUGS

Alice says her drug use began in eighth grade.

"That year, it seemed like a lot of the kids were trying pot," she says. "It didn't seem like a big deal because so many kids were

A recovering addict, Alice now shares sodas with friends instead of alcohol. She says she began drinking as a child because she liked the taste of liquor and found it easy to sneak drinks.

doing it. The first time for me, I was at my friend's house. She had some people over, kind of a party. My two best friends and I left—we had a joint and wanted to try it, but we didn't want to have any boys around in case we did it wrong. We didn't want to look stupid.

"So we went out to the alley and smoked it. I got crabby because I wasn't high. I was really disappointed—it wasn't anything! I kept saying, 'This is so stupid. I'm not high—I'm not even a little bit high.' But my friend told us that we should start running; running would make the joint start working.

"So we started running up and down the alley. By the time we got back to her house, I was so high I couldn't walk straight. I remember sitting in her bedroom and looking around at people I knew, and asking them what their names were and throwing ice cream on her bedroom walls, stupid things like that."

Alice says that she didn't smoke any more pot for several months.

"It wasn't really something I wanted to do all the time, at least not back then," she says. "It just seemed kind of cool. And no, it doesn't seem strange that someone like me, who had lots of friends and was in all these activities would be smoking pot. *Lots* of popular, busy kids were doing that. It was like a double life—we did all these good things, played on teams, and obeyed our parents most of the time, but we drank and smoked pot sometimes, too. You can do that if you are a good liar, unfortunately."

ESCAPING REALITY

Alice's drug and alcohol use increased as she got to high school, and she says there's an easy answer to the question "why?"

"I like drinking," she says. "I like taking drugs. By the time I was in high school, I got high because it was an escape from reality. Like I said before, I didn't like reality. Reality was being depressed and feeling ugly and fat and having no self-esteem.

"I have never been overweight," she says incredulously. "But some people at school would say I was fat, and I believed it! It's amazing how the bad stuff is so easy to believe. I mean, I had it in my mind that anyone who told me something nice was lying to me. I would look around at my friends, and they seemed so beautiful. And then I'd look at myself, and I'd believe how ugly and fat I was.

"So I was depressed, and in my mind, getting high helped me forget all that bad stuff. I didn't have anyone to talk to. Rose didn't get it, and none of my friends would have been able to relate to me. Besides, like I said, they were all beautiful. I wrote a lot of poetry; kept a journal. It didn't really help; it was just a hard, hard time for me."

DRINKING THROUGH THE SCHOOL DAY

Alice admits that she hardly attended classes at all in high school.

"I'd go to school, then leave and go drink," she says. "I'd go to someone's house or go sit in a car or walk to the creek and sit around outside. And this was real drinking, not the stuff we'd do at parties. And these weren't my same friends, either, because none of them needed to drink the way I needed to drink.

"I had a drinking friend for this—she wasn't beautiful, but she was confident. I could relax with her. She had the same opinions about how worthless school was—we were in total agreement about it."

Occasionally, Alice remembers, they didn't even leave school to drink.

"It's so easy," she says, shaking her head. "In school, everyone is drinking coffee to stay awake. Everyone's got one of those plastic mugs, you know? You just put your liquor in there and who's to know? Or you carry a water bottle and fill it with vodka—it's clear, just like water. Nobody suspects, unless you act strangely, and you just don't. Keep to yourself.

"But mostly we'd skip school. We'd head to the liquor stores and hang around outside and ask people to buy us a bottle. It's so easy if you're a girl. We'd pay them an extra five bucks sometimes or buy them a forty-ounce beer. Bums are always willing to do it. And no, nobody gave us any trouble or reported us or anything."

MANIPULATING TEACHERS

Didn't she get in trouble at school for her constant absences? Alice frowns.

"It's different now, but then—no. Back a couple of years ago, if a parent wanted to have their kid on a monitoring system—where the school calls to let them know when the kid is skipping—you had to sign up for it. It wasn't automatic, like now. And I made sure my mom never knew about signing up for that monitoring plan—are you kidding?

"So days would go by and I didn't show up. Sometimes I'd go and a teacher would give me a hard time, but I always had an excuse. That's the number one rule of manipulating—you've got to be ready. I had favorite excuses, the ones that would always work. I'd say, 'I've been dealing with a lot of issues, and I was talking to the counselor.' Or, 'I was working out my schedule with Miss So-and-So.' You have to play one against the other, alternate. You can't use the same person as your excuse too often or you'll get caught."

Although she missed a great deal of school, Alice says she had no intention of flunking her classes.

While in school, Alice says she was adept at manipulating teachers and other adults, so she never got in trouble for skipping classes and managed to earn passing grades.

"I showed up just often enough to know what was going on. Like if a big project was due," she says, "I'd slap the assignment together and slide it under the teacher's door. I'd put a note on it like, 'Sorry, I can't make class today.' More manipulation, you bet. And so I passed my classes; just did just enough to get by. I didn't get good grades, just C's mostly."

IN DEEPER AND DEEPER

As her sophomore year progressed, Alice found herself drinking more than ever. She also had expanded her use of drugs.

"It was pretty bad," she acknowledges. "I was using some prescription drugs I'd gotten when I had knee surgery. And for a few weeks my friend and I were taking these pills her mother had. Her mom had been diagnosed with all sorts of things—multiple personalities, clinical depression, she was manic—like about eighty different things going on with her.

"The drug was called Kronaphin, I think. We heard about it over the Internet. We found out you can break it up and sniff it like cocaine, you know?"

Alice smiles regretfully. "What you can learn surfing the net, huh? Anyway, we'd take lines of that, then drink, then smoke pot. You're not supposed to do all of that together, of course. Actually, you can die from doing that. But it gives you an immense high. And basically it's the same feeling you get when you shoot heroin, I'm told.

"It's a really powerful escape from reality," she continues. "And that was the point, right? But the thing about that was it was really addicting, so we only did it for a few weeks. Mostly it was a lot of pot and alcohol."

Alice says that she needed more money for her increased usage, and that presented a problem.

"I wasn't really working," she says. "But I really needed the money. So I ended up stealing from my parents—a lot. I took their cash card. They found out, sure. I mean, you don't just suddenly come up eight hundred dollars short without wondering why. They were angry; they cut up their cash card and grounded me. Again, they had no idea of the extent of what was going on. It was like a one-time thing, they figured. They were disappointed in me but had no idea how deep I had gone into my addictions. Even with all the drinking and drug use, I hadn't lost my ability to manipulate, to lie."

A Threat Taken Seriously

By the end of her sophomore year in high school, Alice had slid into a deep depression, continuing a cycle of drug and alcohol abuse.

"At the end of the school year my depression was so bad I threatened suicide," Alice says quietly. "I had told my friend I was considering it; I had these prescription drugs from knee surgery that I wanted her to hold for me. I told her that I was worried that if I kept them, I'd be tempted to take them all.

"And she panicked. She went to the principal and told him. I found out when the counselor and the assistant principal tricked me into going to the office one day—they got me there and told me I was going to the psyche ward!"

Alice says she was furious with her friend for betraying her.

"I couldn't believe it," she says. "They carried me—*carried me*—out to the assistant principal's car. I was kicking and screaming, crying, fighting. They called my parents, and they met us at the hospital.

"My parents' reaction?" She smiles sardonically. "My mom was angry with me at first, I think. She thought I was being very self-ish. It wasn't a good reaction, not good at all. My dad was really upset, though. He felt terrible. But they gave their consent for me to be checked into the hospital."

Once checked into the ward, Alice admits, she fell back on her ability to fool people to get what she wanted.

"I lied, basically," she says with a shrug. "I told the staff workers there that it was all a mistake—that I never had used drugs, and my depression was nothing more than a temporary kind of low. They believed me, too. I was out within five days. And the therapist I'd been seeing all along—I lied to him, too."

Last Summer

Soon after her release from the hospital, Alice was back to using drugs and drinking again.

"I had a new circle of friends; I just dropped my old ones I'd had from all the activities I'd been in," she says. "There were a billion places we could go, so there was never a worry we'd be found out by our parents. We'd go from car to car, park to park, and—when parents weren't around—from house to house. I was able to keep my parents in the dark about how bad it was, too.

As Alice's drug and alcohol abuse increased, she says she resorted to taking large quantities of powerful prescription drugs, stealing money from her parents, and even considered committing suicide.

"Every once in a while I'd come home drunk and it was the 'Well, she's a teenager' type of thing. They'd been through an episode or two with Rose—although, like I said before, she was a social-user only, nothing like me. But they must have figured that Rose turned out okay, so it was probably just a little phase I was in, too.

"But things got worse and worse. I started sneaking out of my house at night once in a while. I ran away from home for a few days. The worst thing was what happened one night when I drove this guy home; I went inside his house to have a couple of beers and ended up getting raped by him."

CHECKING HERSELF BACK IN

Alice's self-assurance falters, and her voice breaks.

"I don't know—I wasn't drunk or anything. I didn't expect it, never saw it coming. I'd known this guy since I was little, but he wasn't a real friend or anything. He was an extremely powerful person—lots of drugs, lots of alcohol, lots of cash around. It was drug money, sure. That's what he did.

"But rape? I never thought it would happen to me, and I felt terrible. I drove back to a friend's house and grabbed a knife from her kitchen. I got in my car and started cutting up my wrists, just stabbing at them. I drove myself to that same hospital I'd been in before and checked myself in. I could have checked in without hurting myself, I know—but in my mind, it seemed like the best thing at the time.

"I remember that night very well. The staff at the hospital had to get in touch with a parent—that's the policy. My mom was in Florida at the time; my dad was home. But see, he's got a hearing problem and didn't hear the phone ringing. Remember, it was like 4:00 in the morning.

"So they called my mom in Florida. It must have been really horrible for her, being so far away and hearing this news about her daughter. There I was, standing in the hospital lobby bleeding all over the place. And all the while I'm hiding this big knife in my sleeve—like I thought I'd sneak it into the psych ward!"

Alice laughs, shaking her head.

"I WAS JUST TIRED OF BEING THE WAY I WAS"

"I stayed in the hospital a month that time," she says. "And this time I was ready to be honest. I told them everything I'd lied about before—especially about the drugs I'd been taking. I also told my mom and dad about being raped. And finally I told them about the sexual abuse that happened back when I was kidnapped.

"At that point, I wasn't manipulating at all. I was just tired of being the way I was. I was in so much pain, and I didn't like being that way. And my parents were trying—really *trying*—to be understanding. It was a lot of information to throw at them at one time.

And I understood that it had been a mistake to have kept that information to myself—it helped no one."

When she was finally released from the hospital, Alice was determined that she was going to stay clean and sober.

"Like I said, I was tired of being that other person, the one who lied to her parents, who drank and took drugs. But it didn't work for me that time. I wanted it to, but it didn't."

"I Need Help!"

Alice started going to parties and, although she told herself she would not drink or smoke pot, it was too easy to backslide.

"At first I was doing okay," she says, "but I ended up using as much as before. Then the whole cycle started again, sneaking out of the house, lying to my parents. I wasn't drinking as much as I was smoking pot. And I was feeling those same emotions again—feeling depressed and upset. I felt inferior to everyone. And with those feelings came that same self-destructive feeling, like I wanted to die."

One evening Alice made a telephone call to one of the doctors she'd met at the hospital. He had seemed particularly caring, she says.

"He was a really nice doctor, a good guy who seemed to really understand," she explains. "I told him that things weren't going at all well. I told him I really needed a treatment program or something, so I could function outside the hospital. And he understood. He told me I should call him the next morning when he was in his office and we'd talk about a program that would work for me."

Later that night, however, things took a turn for the worst. Alice's depression and suicidal feelings were stronger, and she knew she didn't want to wait until morning.

"I could have killed myself that night," she admits. "I knew that was a possibility. But instead of doing that, I took my dad's car and drove to the hospital. I didn't go in, because I knew that doctor wouldn't be in yet. I think he was due in at nine or something.

"So I sat in that parking lot, just waiting for him to start his shift. I figured this way he'd have to deal with me because I'd be there in person. And I was right! He came in and I was right there. 'I need help!' I said to him."

"I Was Serious This Time"

Alice says that it was obvious to anyone who saw her that morning that she was in trouble.

Although clean and sober now, Alice realizes that her battle with substance abuse is far from over and she must avoid behavior that might put her at risk for resuming her addiction.

"I looked awful," she says. "I was pale, skinny, frail, and really gross. I hadn't been eating anything; basically, I had been trying to kill myself with drugs and alcohol the previous week. I told him that I was serious this time, that I was through with the way I'd been living. All the doctor had to do was look at me for a second, and he'd know he had to deal with me.

"He did, too. We sat down and he set me up with a treatment program just west of here. And so I started that right away, and it was really intense—*really* intense. I started last October 25."

Alice exhales a deep breath and takes a long drink of her pop.

"It was three months, all day long. I'd come home at night to sleep, then right back there the next day. It was really controlled; we had urinalysis every week, or sometimes every other week, depending on how much the staff trusted us. A very strict contract—I mean, if we weren't serious about getting better, they weren't going to baby us. We didn't have lots and lots of chances. We were out if we screwed up."

RETURNING, AND LEAVING

Alice says that she "graduated" to the continued outpatient program in January of last year.

"I knew my addiction wasn't over," she says, "because it never really is. But I started in the continued outpatient program, which meant I could return to high school. So that's what I did—started back last January.

"Even though it seemed like the right thing to do, it was a mistake for me to return to my high school. I mean, during the first two weeks back, I think I went to about five classes in that time. And considering there are six classes in a day, and I was there ten days, that's not so good. As I mentioned before, I did not use during that time, but I skipped classes and just walked around until I found someone I used to hang out with or someone I used to do drugs with, and then I'd hang out with them.

"I had *no* problem at all getting out of class," she smiles, a little embarrassed. "It was the same old me, manipulating the teachers and counselors. This time I'd tell them I felt like I was going to have a nervous breakdown, or I was going to have a relapse, or I really needed to talk to my counselor. And since they all knew my history, they believed me. I think they were scared that I was going to just fly apart in their classrooms, and they sure didn't want that. Nobody did.

"So off I'd go, walking around. And it was dawning on me that I was in a bad pattern of behavior, that even though I wasn't actually drinking or using drugs, I was very close to it. I was putting myself in risky behavior, and that was just asking for trouble. So it was decided I'd drop out. And so I did, at the end of January."

A Life Outside of School

Alice says it did not feel strange being out of school on the days her peers were there, taking tests, doing reports, participating on teams.

"Don't forget, I hadn't been at school much over the last two years," she smiles. "I'd been in treatment, or I'd been skipping class or something else. It has been a long time since school was a real part of my routine.

"It didn't take long for me to figure out a new routine. I have continued in the outpatient part of my treatment program. I got a job at a pizza place, not too far from where I go for treatment. And this coming Saturday I'll have six months of sobriety," she announces proudly.

"It's almost a cliché, about taking your life one day at a time, but it's very true. I don't know that I ever really tried to make long-range plans—maybe when I was little, but I don't remember—but I sure don't engage in that now. My job is fun, but I know it's not my career. I want to have something meaningful in my life; but right now, I don't know what that may be.

"There's this place called Sobriety High—it's a really small high school for people who have been through the kind of treatment I've been through. That makes more sense to me than trying to go back to a regular high school, so I think that's what I'll do. Sobriety High can only take forty-four kids at a time, and they're full now. I'm on a waiting list; hopefully by next fall there will be a spot for me."

Alice smiles a little sadly.

"Sometimes I have these strong feelings that I want to do school-type things; some days I don't even want to think about it. I get up, go to work, talk to my friends—it often seems like school is something I don't have time for. I want to get my diploma, though, so probably I'll be going to school at some point in the near future. And who knows? Maybe I'll enjoy that so much I'll keep going. Maybe I'd enjoy something in theater or music if I went on to college."

She shakes her head, as though coming out of a dream.

"Wow, did I just say 'college'?" she laughs. "I'm really getting ahead of myself, aren't I?"

"I Don't Blame Anybody"

Alice says she considers herself a very changed person—and a very lucky one.

"I've gotten sort of a new chance at things," she says. "I've got lots of friends—mostly people I've met in treatment or other sober friends. I have a pretty wide circle, and that's good. I don't associate anymore with those kids I used to drink or do drugs with. They—including that guy who raped me—are still doing what they've been doing. I just stay far away.

"I've gotten a lot closer to my parents through all of this, too. My dad and I get along better than my mom and I do, but I guess

Alice now works at a restaurant. "My job is fun," she says, "but I know it's not my career. I want to have something meaningful in my life."

Alice isn't resentful about the events that have led to her dropping out of school. Her hardships have taught her valuable lessons and have even strengthened her relationship with her father and her involvement with her church.

that's just the way it will always be. We're just more alike. He and I do things together more than we ever did—cross-country skiing in the winter, movies, just talk. I'm more active in church now—I'm even an acolyte!

"When I think about all the things that have gone on, that have caused me to drop out of my school, I don't really get angry. Maybe it seems as though I should, but I don't. I mean, who would

I get angry at? I don't blame anybody—it doesn't help. That's like looking backwards, you can't move forward if you're looking in your rearview mirror, right?

"It's nobody's fault; things just happen. The way I look at it, God has a plan for everyone. My plan is a little jagged, but I'll get to where I need to go, eventually."

David

"IF I'D STAYED IN SCHOOL, STAYED
AWAY FROM THOSE GANGS . . .
THINGS WOULD HAVE BEEN
DIFFERENT FOR ME, DIFFERENT
FOR MY FATHER. HE WOULDN'T
HAVE BEEN ANGRY WITH ME, AND
I WOULDN'T BE CUT OFF FROM
HIM NOW."

*Author's Note: David, at eighteen, is definitely a survivor. He was the tar-
get of attempted murder at the hands of gang members, yet lived to testify
against his attackers. No longer a part of a gang, David is engaged and is
looking forward to becoming a father in a few months. His luck has not ex-
tended to his education, however. He left high school at fifteen, then far
more interested in the gang life than in schoolwork. He realizes now, as he
looks for steady employment, how few choices he has without a diploma. It
is easy to blame David for the poor choices he made in high school. However, his family life was also to blame; his father's new wife made it clear
that she disliked David and his siblings almost immediately. David was
on his own physically and emotionally at an age when young people need
their parents' support the most. It's difficult to imagine this smiling,
thoughtful young man wielding an automatic weapon at the age of fifteen.*

If you knew him a couple of years ago, David says with a shrug of
his shoulders, you wouldn't have wanted to have much to do with
him. He was a gangbanger—not *just* a gangbanger, but the num-
ber-two man in the Tiny Man Crew, or TMC.

But today, on a warm May morning, sitting in the park with the
sun on his face, the stocky eighteen-year-old hardly looks the part

of a menacing gang member. He is relaxed and smiling, leaning casually against the back of a picnic table. His voice is quiet and polite, and he is very candid about the events that led to his dropping out of school three years ago.

"Start with My Family"

"It's pretty impossible to understand about me unless you start with my family," he says with an edge to his voice. "I'm sure that's true with almost anyone, right? Our families have a lot to do with who we are, or how we act.

"I have nine brothers and sisters. I grew up in the city here. My mom died when I was a month old; she had a nose bleed that wouldn't stop. I don't know what the cause of it was, or why they couldn't stop the bleeding, but that's what happened. What I've heard as I grew up was just little bits and pieces since no one talks much about it. The doctors just couldn't do anything.

"My father was seventy when I was born—he's eighty-seven now! He and my mother came from Thailand; that's where my older brothers and sister were born. My father was the right-hand man to an important general in South Vietnam and fought in the war there against North Vietnam. When my mother was pregnant with me they moved to Australia, and that's where I was born. And that is where she died."

"Good Memories of My Dad"

David says that his father remained in Australia for two years, taking care of his four young children.

"He was real lonely for my mom," he says. "I don't remember much, but I know that's why we ended up coming to the United States. Australia was really pretty and everything, but it reminded him of her. So we started all over here in America.

"I don't see my father anymore," he says sadly. "He won't let me talk to him—I haven't seen him in two years. He doesn't like me anymore. I guess that comes later in the story. But I *do* have very good memories of my dad when I was growing up, before all the trouble started.

"Like I said, he was pretty old even then, when I was little. But he loved me—at least then he did. I can remember, before I was old enough to start school, walking with him to the store and him

Just a few years ago, eighteen-year-old David was an active member in the Tiny Man Crew, an Asian gang in his neighborhood.

carrying a hundred-pound sack of rice on his shoulders but still holding my hand. I think of that as how a father should be. He's a good man, a real good man.

"We lived a Hmong life here. We ate mostly Hmong, spoke that language at home. My dad speaks three languages—Hmong, Thai, and some English, but he chose not to speak English at home. That is learned just out on the street or later at school. He didn't have to work because he was retired and had a good pension from the army. So that meant he could be home with us all the time. He did all the cooking and the cleaning for us—and life was pretty happy for a while."

GOING TO SCHOOL

David's early school experiences were mostly pleasant, he says.

"I liked going," he says. "I had ESL, English as a Second Language. There was a language specialist who spoke Hmong and English who would work with us for a couple hours each day, to help us get caught up with English.

"Science was fun, too. We had microscopes in our classroom and a guinea pig and lots of books. I wasn't a very good reader then, but I liked looking at some of those books. Our teacher was good, especially in fifth grade. We'd study about germs and bacteria, and we'd look at some in the microscopes. If I had stayed in school, I bet I would have concentrated on science stuff. Maybe I would have been good at it—who knows? I'm not very good at anything now."

It was during David's elementary school years that his father got remarried. It was a complete surprise to him as well as his brothers and sister, he says.

"He went down to Iowa to celebrate the Hmong New Year—I guess with some friends down there," says David. "Us kids stayed home, and relatives that lived nearby watched us. I was about eight, I think. He was gone a month, and when he came back he told us that we were going to move to an apartment and that he was getting married."

"SHE JUST DIDN'T LIKE US"

"The lady he married had three small kids," he explains. "And there were four of us, my dad's kids. Eventually she and my dad had two more of their own. They call that a blended family, I guess. It wasn't such a good blend, though.

"We didn't really have much to do with her kids. Her oldest was a girl, younger than me. And she was—what do you call it?—mentally retarded. And the boy—all he did was draw and read comic books. Never talked to anybody, so he wasn't much fun. And then there was a real little girl, just a baby.

"I don't think my stepmother was bad at first. I actually remember being sort of happy that we were moving because some of our cousins lived in the same apartment building, and it would be fun having them nearby. But after a while, it didn't help that we had family there because our own family life was getting really terrible.

"My stepmother started off kind of nice, but after a little while she started hitting us. I say 'us'—I mean my brothers and my sister and me. Her own kids, she didn't hit. It was a lot, yeah. We'd get hit for running around inside, or for playing with one of her kid's toys. Or especially if we wanted something to eat. She just didn't like us; that was the whole thing. It was so different from the way my dad had been! And it got worse— way worse."

David says his life changed drastically after his father remarried. As his family life deteriorated, David started associating with gang members.

David says he doesn't think he and his siblings offended his stepmother.

"At least I don't remember doing that," he says. "I mean, we weren't perfect, but we were just kids. But she'd say mean things to us, insult us. And she'd talk about us in bad ways—right in front of us, as though we weren't even there! And later on, after she and my dad had children of their own together, it got worse. One of the worst things she'd do is hide food from us. We would be hungry, looking for anything at all to eat, and she'd scream at us to leave the kitchen, to get out."

"HE DIDN'T WANT HER TO LEAVE"

He tried to talk to his father about it, David says, but it didn't seem to do any good.

"My father is old," he shrugs. "And he knew we were being mistreated, but he must have seen a different side of her. He was unwilling to start a fight with her because he didn't want her to leave. If she left, she'd take the babies with her, and my dad didn't want that. She was a lot younger than him, and she could really make him do about anything. He bought her a new car, new stuff for the apartment—anything she wanted.

"But us kids—we were on the bottom, as far as she was concerned. She'd never buy us anything new, but she'd buy her own kids everything. And by the time I was in junior high, it was so bad that she was actually locking the freezer so we couldn't get food. If we went out and bought our own, she'd have a fit, make us get out of the kitchen."

DOWNHILL AT SCHOOL

Things weren't much better at school, either. By the time David was in junior high, he had started associating with a gang.

"It was different in junior high," he admits. "The Asian kids sort of hung together, apart from the other kids. Things just got separate. The Hmong kids would band together back in grade school a little bit, but lots of times that was just because some of us were more comfortable not speaking English. But I don't think I ever felt that we *couldn't* have hung around the other kids.

"In junior high, though, we were really apart. I liked these Asian kids who were in gangs—most of them belonged to the Tiny Man Crew, or TMC. They were sort of the Asian set of the Bloods gang. I don't really remember how I started hanging with them—I know I thought they were cool because they were smoking outside of school. I started wearing baggy clothes like they had, and it just went on from there.

"Not all the Asian kids were in the TMC; some of them were Crips. So we'd get in fights with them. I started getting suspensions, which I'd never done before. They'd be like three-day suspensions for fighting. It seemed like there were so many fights—every afternoon. And once a week it seems like I had a suspension."

JUVENILE DETENTION

Most of the fights at school were fistfights, but occasionally there were more serious altercations.

"One time one of the Crips brought a gun to school. That would happen every so often, I guess. But it was stupid because you can't get the gun past the teachers in the hallway. It seemed like the teachers were always busy, trying to keep our gangs apart all the time. It wasn't just outside, either. We had fights inside the school, in the halls, even in the classrooms.

"I was in a big fight one time in a classroom. We ended up throwing desks and everything. The teacher was up there talking, you know, and one of the Crips turns around and throws some gang sign. Then one of our guys threw one. And the Crip gets up, and we get up, and all of a sudden we're all talking crap, you know. And then somebody throws a punch, and it gets out of hand. Pretty soon we're throwing garbage cans and desks.

"That time it was bad, and the cops got called. We all got arrested, a whole bunch of us. I think there were ten of us TMCs and two Crips. We didn't have to stay, though. The Crips had knives on them, so they were the ones that got in big trouble."

NEEDING HIS FATHER

David says that when he got suspensions, he always hoped his father would be the one to come to school to pick him up.

"They got a rule that your parents are supposed to come get you when you get a detention," he explains. "They talk to the counselor or the principal or whoever; just so the school knows that your family knows what's going on. But my dad never would come. Instead, he'd send my older brother Kou. He's eight years older than me—he's a pilot now. But he'd be the one to come and get me.

"That would hurt my feelings, I guess you'd say. It seemed like he didn't care enough to come see what was going on. I'd get home and my stepmother would start yelling at me, and then I'd get into a yelling match with her. It always seemed like at home I was going around feeling mad or sad, or both."

While David was getting in trouble at school, his father showed little interest in him, which caused David to become both sad and frustrated.

David says that Kou would try to talk to him about his behavior, but it had no effect on him.

"Kou would get in my face, you know, tell me about how stupid I was to get involved with the gangs, how I was going to get killed. But I wouldn't listen to him. Now, I look back, I wish I had listened because things would have been different."

BARELY PASSING

The quality of his schoolwork fell as his gang activity increased, David remembers.

"Ninth grade, it seemed like I was just getting by," he says. "I wasn't turning in homework usually; if there was something really important I had to do, my sister or my brother would help me get it done. It didn't seem very important, not compared to the stuff I was doing in real life, you know?

"Like, when I was fourteen, I got initiated as the second in command of TMC. That's a pretty high rank, you know? They didn't call me David in the gang—my name was Hammer Junior. There was already a Hammer who was an older gangster, so that's why I got the 'junior' part added. The guy who had had the rank before me got arrested. He killed somebody, so he's serving a life sentence now.

"Anyway, things just seemed to get pretty exciting, especially that summer between ninth and tenth grades. I was hanging around a lot at this one housing project—that's where most of the TMC boys were from.

"My dad knew I was spending less time doing the things I should be doing, too. He wasn't sure exactly *what* was going on, but he knew I wasn't doing much schoolwork. And he knew I was being disobedient to him; in our house, there was no excuse for that.

"One time he got really mad at me because I had stayed overnight at a friend's house without calling home and telling him. I was just into my friends, you know, into the gang. Well anyway, I got home later the next day, and my dad got so mad he put a curse on me."

THE CURSE

David notes my quizzical expression and explains that in his religion, Buddhism, there are very specific curses that parents can put on children as punishment for misbehavior.

"The one he put on me was bad," he says. "It sounds kind of mean, but I know I had it coming. And even then, while he was doing it, I knew I deserved it, even though it made me mad. My older brother and my dad jumped me when I came home and tied me up like you'd tie up a pig you were going to slaughter. There was a rope tied around my hands, and there was one tied around my neck that connected to my ankles. The more I would move, the tighter the rope would be around my neck, that's the idea.

"Well, I couldn't really move, and my dad took a sharp knife and cut off my hair. I had long hair then, down to about my armpits. I had it in a ponytail and had the sides of my head shaved, like a lot of the guys in the gang.

"He burned the hair and said some words I don't know how to translate. And that was it. The next day, I knew what would happen—I couldn't leave the house or I'd get sick. I tried opening the door, but my stomach would hurt so much that I couldn't even move. The curse lasted a whole day. And man—my stomach hurt so much, I can't even describe it. Just thinking about leaving home would start the pains again."

David seems surprised that some might doubt the validity of such a curse.

"I don't know," he shrugs. "But it worked on me. I have no trouble believing in it; it worked on me."

"I WAS LYING"

Although he was a little more obedient immediately after the curse, David says it didn't take long for him to backslide again.

"By tenth grade—sophomore year—I was into that gang again; that's like *all* I did. The gang was like my family, more than my real family. I started spending every minute I could with them. 'Cause, why would I want to be home? I'd break into cars; steal stuff. We went to Wisconsin and broke into a gun shop in Green Bay and stole a bunch of guns. Then we came back and made money selling them. I had a .38 special and a .9 Glock.

"You may not believe this, but it's true—we even had three hand grenades that we hid. There was this one guy in our gang that got them and hid them in a secret place. He was the only one who knew where he hid them, and he got killed by his own brother over a video game. So now, nobody knows where they are."

David admits that he was selling drugs, too.

"I didn't take them, but I sold them," he says. "Crack, weed, acid. Sometimes weed and acid mixed together. I never got caught. Sometimes I could make thirteen hundred dollars in a day selling at the projects. Lots of customers over there. And about a thousand dollars of it was profit.

"I spent the money on stupid stuff, and it's funny how fast that money can go. It sounds like a lot, but it disappears fast. I'd go out to eat—take a bunch of my friends to a Thai restaurant and order everything on the menu. I'd buy presents for friends, clothes, go to lots of movies. I have nothing to show for it now. Maybe that's good," he adds.

David says that although he was a high-ranking gang member, he was still able to convince his father that he was not involved with gangs.

"I told him all along that I wasn't in a gang; I was lying. I think he believed me," says David, thinking. "Maybe he knew, but he didn't argue about it. He seemed to accept what I told him. Maybe he just wanted to pretend that I had more sense than to do that stuff, I don't know."

NO SCHOOL AT ALL

David was not going to school during this time; however, he had no trouble with the truant officers.

"I was only fifteen at the time," he says. "And you know that law supposedly that you have to be in school until you're sixteen? Complete BS. It was the middle of my sophomore year, and I never went. I'd given wrong phone numbers on my school emergency card, and if they came around to the house, I guess my father would have just said that he didn't know where I was, which would have been true.

"Plus, it's different when you're Hmong. In lots of Hmong families, the parents couldn't speak any English. How hard do you think the school tried to look up a kid who was skipping?

"So instead, I was on the streets with my friends. We started up a new gang—called it OHB, Oriental Hmong Blood. It was even bigger; we had lots of Asian guys from a lot of different high schools around here who wanted to be in it. I was the leader of the OHBs, and we made sure everybody was protected. We hung out over at the Plaza projects, and then over on Western, at some projects over there.

David was the leader of the Oriental Hmong Blood during his gang days. Today, however, he leads a more peaceful life, opting to participate in baseball games rather than gang activities.

"There were cops at the project—hey, there was even a cop station over there! But they were on the other side from where we hung out, and they didn't even see what was happening until it was over most of the time. Like some Crips would come driving in, by the projects. And we knew their cars. And we'd start shooting right away. Usually by the time the cops were called the excitement was over.

"I was staying away from home more and more, too, even at night. I was in motels sometimes, sometimes just couch hopping, going from the house of one friend to another."

JAIL

It was during that time that David's father was faced with undeniable evidence of his son's gang activities.

"I was in jail," he says. "There had been a drive-by over at the projects; about half of us got caught and taken downtown. The police called my dad, and this time he found out plenty—more than he really wanted to know, I guess. Like I said before, I'd been lying to him. And sometimes I felt really bad about it.

"Like there'd be times when another gang would find out where I lived, and they'd smash some windows, or write on the outside walls, or try to break in and scare them. And I'd always say, 'It's some guys in a gang that are trying to get me to join, but I'm not going to'—something like that. It was my fault, and I'd feel guilty that they were getting frightened like that because of me.

"But now, my dad knew. And he told me he never wanted me in the house again, not for anything. He said he and my stepmother would call the cops on me if I did show up. And so I said, fine, I wouldn't be coming around; so that was that.

THINKING ABOUT THINGS

David says that he was both angry and disappointed at his father's decision to ban him from the house.

"Even though I had been gone a lot, hanging around with the gang, it felt really strange for him to make an order like that—it was so final. And after a few hours of being really angry with him, I started feeling really sad.

"I started thinking really hard about things. I was thinking about how it was when I was little, when we lived in Australia. And I kept picturing in my mind the way my dad was a good dad then. I thought about how he had us four little kids after my mom died, and how he tried so hard to raise us. He never had any smoking or drinking in the house; he probably never thought any of us would grow up to be disrespectful to him. Did he think I would become a gangbanger, stealing and selling drugs, or shooting at people? I thought about how he never imagined he'd be tying me up, putting that curse on me, cutting off my hair with a big knife."

David's eyes fill with tears, and he clumsily wipes them with the back of his hand.

"I remember being two or three years old and sitting by the window with him. He was talking about my mom, and what a nice lady she was and how he missed her. He started crying, and then I started crying. I hugged him, and he felt better. He'd touch my head and talk to me. I remember really well how I didn't know the words to say, because I was too young.

David's father banished him from his home after learning of David's gang involvement. "After a few hours of being really angry with him," David recalls, "I started feeling really sad."

"And then I started thinking about when we moved here, before he got married again. We'd have these water fights in the yard. My brothers and I would have water balloons, and we'd throw them at my dad. He had the hose, and he'd laugh when he squirted us."

He smiles. "I didn't know what I was going to do when I was thinking about all this stuff. I mean, I know that as you grow up there are changes. You can't stay the same forever. But I was wishing that I had enjoyed it more while I had it. Thinking like that was kind of sad, but in a way it was good. It was nice remembering the time back then when he loved me, and I loved him."

A DECISION, AND A PROBLEM

It was just two days after he was released from jail, David says, that he came to a decision.

"I remember it was my birthday," he says. "My sweet sixteenth—but it wasn't so sweet. I decided to get out of the gang. I'd met this one guy we called McFly—that was his nickname. He'd been a TMC before, but he'd gotten married and wasn't having anything to do with the gang anymore. They let him alone, I guess. Usually gangs don't like to have people leave, and they give you a real bad time.

"McFly introduced me to his cousin, who wasn't in a gang, either. I'd left the neighborhood I'd been hanging around and was hanging around with him instead, just getting my head straight, thinking about things. I knew I wanted to change, but it was a question of how, you know?

"Anyway, that day I saw two TMC guys coming toward me. I got real nervous because I didn't know what they were up to. They told me they wanted me to go back to the projects with them so they could jump me out of the gang. Well, I figured one of two things was going to happen to me—I'd get shot, or I'd get beaten half to death."

ATTEMPTED MURDER

David started arguing with the two, explaining that he really couldn't leave.

"They started arguing with me, telling me I didn't have much of a choice," he says. "And I was getting more and more scared. I threw a punch, hit one of the guys in the side of his head, and I started running. I saw a security guard and told him I was being chased, but he didn't want to help me—I think he was scared. I was begging him, you know, but no way.

"Those guys caught up to me and grabbed me. They were going to stuff me in the trunk of the car, but when they opened it there was too much junk back there. Plus, I'm sort of big. Anyway, they decided to put me in the front seat. And I was afraid then because that's when I saw the one guy had a gun. I saw it in the waistband of his pants when he lifted his shirt up to scratch his stomach or something."

David says that they drove onto the interstate, heading back to the projects. He knew he had to get out of the car, and fast.

"We were just getting on the highway from the ramp," he says, "and I punched the guy driving, real hard. He lost control of the car for a minute and hit the side of the ramp when the car swerved. I opened the car door and jumped out. I thought I'd made it, but he grabbed hold of my T-shirt and hung on."

He shudders. "Of all the times for a T-shirt *not* to rip! I was praying it would, you know, but it didn't. So he steps on the gas; we're going fifty, sixty miles an hour with me dragging outside the car by my T-shirt."

A NARROW ESCAPE

David says that the driver of the car behind them had a cell phone and called 911 when he saw David being dragged alongside the speeding car.

"I don't remember a lot about it," he admits. "My shoes came off, I remember that. I found out later that I'd gotten dragged along the road for about two hundred feet. That's why I'm all burned up, see? And that's why I got these big scars on my hands."

David shows his wrists and forearms, where large round scars are prominent.

"My hands were just flipping back and forth; I was trying to steady myself, trying to get loose. But it hurt so bad, I couldn't do anything at all. That's about as much as I remember. I know the ambulance came, thanks to that guy with the cell phone. And he was able to give the license number of the TMC guy's car, so the police could try to catch up with him later.

"I remember lying there, lifting my hand and seeing the skin just hanging down, bleeding like everything. In the ambulance,

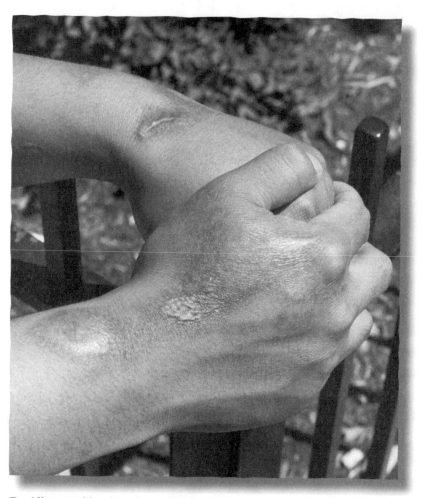

David's scarred hands and arms hint at the dangerous ordeal he endured when he decided to leave the Tiny Man Crew gang. Fellow gang members kidnapped David and attempted to murder him.

I remember just a mask of cold, cold air going in my mouth. I was shivering real bad, even though it was hot outside."

The hospital staff cut off his clothes and immediately gave him morphine for the pain. He stayed in the hospital for about a week.

"There's a lot of stuff they did to help me," he says, "but a lot of stuff they couldn't fix. Like I have nerves that were damaged on my left arm here, so it's completely numb. And my muscle is flat, too—even when I flex it, see? It's hard for me to lift things now. I have to carry them using the strength of my back more than the strength of my arms."

"My Dad Didn't Feel Much Pity"

The police were able to catch the gang member who drove the car. David agreed to press charges.

"I didn't really hesitate to do it," he says. "I mean, they charged him with attempted murder, and that was right. I figured he'd tried to kill me, and probably would do it tomorrow to somebody else. I'd had it with the gang life by then.

"After a stay in the hospital that seemed to go on forever, the police told me I should stay at the juvenile detention center while the court case was going on, sort of like for protection, you know? I guess they wanted to keep me safe since I'd have to testify. The case went on about a month, and they found the guy guilty. They sentenced him to life in prison, too.

After that, the police told me that the best place for me to go to recuperate was home. I was still bandaged up, and it was hard for me to move around. Everything was sore, you know? But my dad didn't feel much pity! I mean, he wouldn't even come to pick me up when I was released. He told me to get my own ride home, and he hung up on me.

"See, he didn't believe me. He figured I was lying to him, telling him I was through with gangs, just like I lied to him back when I told him I wasn't in a gang. So I can't really fault him for turning me down. But this time he was wrong. I was trying to get out of the gang. It's like that story of the boy who cried wolf, you know? You keep lying, and when you finally tell the truth you want to be believed. But I wasn't.

"I went home, yeah. At least he let me stay for a while. He didn't talk to me; my stepmother was still mean. I stayed for two months, and then my brother and I got into a fight. He's the sec- ond oldest—drives a school bus. He started hassling me, telling me to get off my butt and go get a job, do something with my life. I said, 'How can I do that when I'm covered in bandages?' He threw a folding chair at me—you know, one of those metal ones? And then we got into it, fighting in the house.

"My dad came in and got really mad. He blamed me— even though I didn't start it. He said the fight never would have happened if I hadn't been there. And I was the one who got the worst of it—I had a huge black eye!"

"I WAS WORRIED"

David claims that his gang days are long over, although he admits he's had a few tense moments since the trial.

"Now TMC guys don't give me trouble at all," he says. "They talk to me, but no big deal. I was worried at first, when a couple of them started walking over to talk to me when I was at a park right after the trial was over. I saw them coming and I'm like, 'Okay, here goes. I'm going to get shot now.' But it was cool. They just were like, 'Hey, what's up,' and stuff like that.

"Now I'm not a gang member; I will never consider myself a gang member again. I don't throw signs or dress in any gang colors. I'm me. And the one good thing that happened because of the trial is that my dad believes me. He hasn't forgiven me, but at least he knows I'm no longer in a gang. I mean, he had no choice but to figure that out because of my testimony. But he still doesn't like me, doesn't trust me.

"So I'm not allowed at his house. That was two years ago, and he hasn't changed his mind, even though I've asked him to. So for the last two years I've been a homeless person—a homeless person with a family that won't forgive him."

ON HIS OWN

At age sixteen, David was on his own, going from shelters to a group home and finally to his own apartment.

"Some of the shelters were okay," he says. "But they have rules where you can only stay at a shelter a certain amount of time—usually three weeks at the most. So then I'd leave and find another one. Sometimes I was just on the streets.

"After a while I got into this one county program called Project Solo. It helps teens who have no place to stay but who want to work, find a place for themselves. The people at Project Solo helped me get into other shelters—longer term shelters—and even helped me rent an apartment. They pay part of your rent for you.

"I had a job for a while in a Thai restaurant called the Royal Orchid. I was a waiter, and the manager told me when I was hired that I'd get to keep all my tips, plus my wages; but they weren't paying me what I earned. I tried to talk to them about it but they refused. I quit after getting into a disagreement with the manager. I even tried to talk to a lawyer about it, but he said there wasn't much I could do since it was a verbal agreement."

MEETING HEATHER

David signed up at a temporary employment service soon after leaving the restaurant.

"I liked that; you'd get a call that you had a job for a few days in a factory or something. The money's good and it doesn't get too boring since you're always moving to a new location. So I was doing that, earning money and paying my rent. I was starting to feel like maybe I had a future, you know? And then I met Heather."

David smiles happily.

David and his girlfriend, Heather, met in Project Solo, a program that helps homeless teens. "She's the best thing that's ever happened to me," David says.

"She's the best thing that's ever happened to me, really. Heather's had a hard time in her life, just like me. She was in Project Solo, too—that's how we met. So we met, and I kind of liked her—but it was too soon to really tell, you know. And then later that day, I was down at District—that's this center for gay and lesbian teens.

"Now, I'm not gay, and Heather's not a lesbian. That's what made it kind of like fate, I think. I was there with a friend of mine, and she was there with her friend. Two straight people—were we ever surprised to see each other again! We talked some more, and we realized how much we liked each other. And things just progressed from there.

"When we started getting really involved we went down to the Red Door—that's this one clinic where you can be tested for HIV and stuff. We were both fine. So we started really being serious about each other."

David shrugs, as if baffled by the whole thing.

"I've never met anyone like her before. And she thinks the same about *me*! We've got rings; we're going to get married sometime soon. And the best news is that we're having a baby in about two months. I never thought about being a father before, but now I can hardly wait. We know it's a girl already, and we're both excited."

REGRETS

David and Heather will be moving into their own apartment in about a week.

"It's not in a great neighborhood," he says. "It's real close to where that old lady got killed by those crack dealers, remember on the news? But at least we're together, and Heather's out of her mom's house. See, she and her mom don't get along all the time. And her mom really doesn't like me much. So that part's good.

"I'm hoping to find a full-time job soon. I applied for a security position, and I did good on the first interview. But they did a background check on me, and since I had arrests back in my gang days, they turned me down. But there are factories that will take me. I guess I'm limited in what's out there—I don't have a diploma."

David says that he regrets all of the circumstances that led to his leaving school at such a young age.

David searches for a job in the newspaper classifieds. Since dropping out of school, David has held temporary jobs but realizes that his options are limited without a diploma.

"It's partly the idea there are jobs I can't even apply for," he says. "But it isn't just that, not just a money thing. See, me and Heather sometimes go to the library and hang out, and I see these kids come in there from different schools. They've got their backpacks on, and they're doing reports for school."

He smiles shyly. "Man, I miss doing that. I envy them. I feel like learning to use a computer and finding out all about something.

Then I look at myself, no school, no diploma, no nothing. And they're doing it all. I'm sitting there just thumbing through a magazine, just passing time. That's when I get really depressed about things, you know?

"Sometimes I get bored, and I think that if I were in school I'd have more to think about. Now, what I do is I volunteer for things. I help down at District—they always need someone to unpack stuff, carry things. Even though I'm straight, the people there are nice to me. And I volunteer to do studies—I'm signed up to do one

David says he misses school and learning about new subjects. To partially fill this void, David volunteers for university studies, including a current one about smoking addiction.

on the addictiveness of cigarettes they're having at the university. It ought to be fun, and maybe they'll learn something important that will help other people. Maybe it will be famous, and I can tell everybody I was in on it, huh?"

"I DON'T THINK HE'LL EVER FORGIVE ME"

But David's biggest regret in leaving school was the rift it caused in his family.

"If I'd stayed in school, stayed away from those gangs," he says, "things would have been different for me, different for my father. He wouldn't have been angry with me, and I wouldn't be cut off from him now.

"I don't know if he'll ever forgive me. He's a stubborn man. I've been back a few times, and I tried to talk to him. I try to tell my brothers to talk to him for me. He just refuses. Hey, I even got down on my knees and begged him to forgive me and let me come home. But he won't budge.

"The only one who will really talk to me is my five-year-old sister. She's always happy to talk to me when I call there. She tells me what toys she plays with, who her friends are. And she always asks how I am, how I'm feeling."

David sighs. "I want my dad to know about the baby we're going to have. And I'm afraid he's getting so old, and there's so little time for him to forgive me. I don't want him to die hating me. I'd always feel sad about that, my whole life."

Matt

"I LEFT SCHOOL DURING MY
SENIOR YEAR. AND NO, I DON'T
HAVE ANY INTENTION OF GOING
BACK TO HIGH SCHOOL. I'M MOST
LIKELY GOING TO GET MY GED.
. . . BUT HIGH SCHOOL DIDN'T
WORK OUT VERY WELL FOR ME."

Author's Note: It's almost impossible not to like eighteen-year-old Matt, with his infectious grin and dry wit. He is candid about his failure to do well in high school, explaining that when he transferred out of his inner-city school to a suburban college-prep school, he was snubbed or picked on. One wonders, however, if there was more to the story than that. Matt was clearly proud of his racially mixed, urban upbringing, and admits that he might have been a bit "in your face" in showing it. Wearing baggy shirts and sagging pants, Matt says that he was an outcast almost immediately in his new upper-middle-class school environment. Undoubtedly Matt was treated badly, but in his interview, it seems clear that he was at fault, too. He responded to bullying with outbursts of swearing and fighting—thus making it difficult for his teachers to sympathize with his situation.

Matt's social problems were only part of the difficulty he faced throughout high school. He explains that he had a very hard time sitting still when forced to read, and although his teachers suspected a learning disability, specialists were unable to find one. He left school early in his senior year, after having switched to a city high school in his sophomore year. His social difficulties disappeared, but he continued to struggle in almost every class except woodworking—in which he excelled. Today, with a studded tongue, pierced ears, and a variety of large tattoos, Matt is contemplating his GED (General Educational Development) test, and a technical school.

He answers the door in the middle of the day—an eighteen-year-old whose small build and mischievous smile make him look much younger. He's got a pierced ear and the beginnings of a beard. He's wearing baggy jeans, an unbuttoned, oversized plaid shirt, and a white undershirt. A freckled spaniel is close to his heels.

"I'm Matt," he says, sticking out a hand. "And this is Sam I Am, Esquire. I'm not sure exactly where the 'Esquire' part came from, but the 'Sam I Am' is from *Green Eggs and Ham*."

Matt continues to smile, although he appears distracted by something. He moves his tongue carefully around his mouth, frowning slightly.

"Sorry," he says suddenly. "I just got my tongue pierced four days ago, and it still feels weird. Doesn't hurt, just feels funny. Anyway, my mom is coming home in a bit—so don't say anything about it. I haven't told her yet, and I don't think she'll be very happy.

"Anyway, I'm a dropout. I left school during my senior year. And no, I don't have any intention of going back to high school. I'm most likely going to get my GED this summer, because I promised my dad I would. But high school didn't work out very well for me."

"I'VE ALWAYS LIVED HERE"

Matt lives with his parents and his older brother, Nathan, in a middle-class neighborhood on the city's north side—an area that is quite diverse racially. Two black children ride by on bicycles; a Native American woman walks toward the bus stop carrying a lunch box.

"I've always lived here, in this same house," he says, smiling again. "My dad is a meat man down at the big grocery store on Lake Street. He's a really good guy. And my mom works in the deli at another grocery store. She worries too much. Maybe that's a mom thing, but she seems to worry when I've given her no cause to. Like when I get home at night after picking up my best friend, Tony, from work. I tell her I'll be home at about 12:30, and that's exactly when I get home. But when I come in she's nervous, as though I was hours late.

"Anyway, I'm not a drinker; I don't do drugs. I used to smoke, but since I got my tongue pierced I've stopped that. It's been four days without a cigarette—and boy, are my hands shaky!

"I've got a brother, Nathan, who is twenty. He isn't the best of all people. He goes out drinking every night with his friends, and that's about it. I know that because he just doesn't come home, and I'll see him and his friends down at the coffee shop where I work. He just sort of drives around; there's not much going on right now for Nathan. He used to work for this one tobacco shop, but he left it—didn't like the hours they were making him work."

GROWING UP HAPPY

For the most part, Matt says, he has very pleasant memories of growing up in his family.

"It was a lot of fun when I was little," he says. "Right next door here, that was where my friend Dewey lived—my best friend back then. His dad passed away in '95, and they moved out south. But until then, we were always together. We ran with a whole pack of kids, riding our bikes everywhere. Everybody around the neighborhood called me 'Half ounce'—because I was so small.

"Every kid from a mile radius would come over; we'd play war. Whoever got caught had to go sit either on my porch here or over on his steps. There was always stuff to do."

Matt gestures toward the street.

"This is a real mixed neighborhood, more black now than white, I think. But back then it seemed pretty even. Everyone just basically got along—at least that's how I remember it with us kids. There were Hispanics, Asians, blacks, whites—whatever. We'd play basketball—geez, sometimes for twelve hours straight in the summers."

Matt leans back on the sofa and smiles.

"Things were fun, just fun," he says, remembering.

"MY MOM SAYS THAT I LIKED IT"

"I'll be honest," he says. "I can't say that I liked school much by the time I was a senior. In fact, most of high school was pretty bad in my opinion. But my memories of grade school are pretty nice. When we talk about school stuff in our family, my mom says that I liked it.

"I went to a Catholic grade school, just here in the neighborhood. It was called St. Ann's. I remember having lots of friends; it seemed like everybody knew everybody. My parents were real active, volunteering in the church and the school and everything. It was pretty nice.

Matt relaxes on the porch of his home. He recalls fond memories of growing up in a racially mixed neighborhood where he had a ready supply of friends.

"The work? I don't really remember a lot of the stuff we did, but I *do* remember studying Greek mythology. I really liked that. It's interesting, you know, how the Bible says how everything happened—but then there's this whole other explanation for things! It's great! I did projects about the different gods and goddesses; I'd take a box and have Zeus hanging from a string and the other gods around him. He was throwing lightning bolts, I think."

Matt says that he continued at St. Ann's until seventh grade, when the school merged with another Catholic school, St. Margaret Mary's.

"That was when things started getting bad," he says. "Seventh grade was a real bad year. Part of it was the bus situation. Before, when it was St. Ann's, we'd just walk to school. It wasn't that far. But as seventh graders, me and my friends had our morning classes at St. Margaret Mary's, and that was a very long walk."

LESS AND LESS FUN

Matt says that they could have walked to St. Ann's early and caught a shuttle to St. Margaret Mary's, but it was hard to get there at that hour.

"We'd try, but the bus would leave early or sometimes we'd just be late. So mostly what we'd do is just walk to school, down the parkway. We'd be late a lot. Usually we'd stop at the gas station on the way, get a pop or something. And then by the time we got to school the bell had rung, and the teachers were mad. So that was like a strike against us, I guess.

"Another thing that happened that year was the teachers split the classes into ability groups, or whatever they call them. They never divided us up that way before. I wasn't with any of my friends; instead, I was with these kids who were slower learners. The other group, the one where my friends were, they got to go on more field trips and stuff. And their teacher just read from the book and kids caught on. Like for instance, in my math group, the teacher made us work slower, and she helped us more."

Matt says he wasn't angry about the extra help he received, but he felt bad that he was separated from his friends.

"I know they grouped kids how they thought they learned," he says. "But I just don't think they did it right. I don't think I learn slowly—at least I didn't back then. I just didn't like being separated out like that. I wasn't a behavior problem, either—I usually got along good with my teachers."

"IT SEEMED HARD"

Matt says that classes seemed much harder in seventh grade than they had the year before.

"We had six periods in the day," he explains, "and we'd go to different teachers for everything. You started out with your homeroom teacher in the morning, and then you left. And at the end, you'd go back to homeroom. I know that's pretty common, how schools do things for seventh graders, but it seemed hard.

"The classes were taught really fast, it seemed like. Like they just expected us to get it, bang, bang bang."

He pauses, rubbing the stud on his tongue over his top lip.

"I'd get really confused sometimes. Like I already told you, I'm not a slow learner, but it just seemed like lots of the teachers were going way too fast, like they were assuming everybody got it. And everybody didn't.

"The thing that usually saved *me* was that I had a nice homeroom teacher. When I'd go back there at the end of the day, I'd be starting my homework from all my other classes and she could help explain the stuff that was confusing. She really knew how to explain things well, especially in math. I don't think I'd have gotten it at all if it hadn't been for her that year."

A Decision to Change Schools

Matt wasn't the only one who was dissatisfied with the merger of the two schools. Many of the parents of students at his school were unhappy, too.

"I know some of the mothers would get to talking about things with my mom, down at the store where she works," he says. "They'd kind of compare notes on how their kids were doing or they'd fill each other in on problems that the teachers were having up at the school.

"I know my mom wasn't happy about the new priest, either," Matt says. "She didn't think he related well to the people of the parish, especially those from St. Ann's. A lot of families felt left out because he didn't let them help in the same ways they'd helped before. Like the rummage sale—he'd get new people to run it and make the people who'd run it for years feel bad.

"Anyway, this new priest seemed to rub a lot of people the wrong way, I guess. When some of the parents complained about things, the priest would say, 'I'll take care of it, I'll take care of it.' Or the principal would say the same thing. But between the two of them, none of the problems really got solved. As far as myself, I guess that I got mostly C's in seventh grade. I did okay, but just okay, you know? Not great, but not bad, either."

But by the end of the year, Matt's parents had decided that he would not finish his last year at that school. He and several other students were to switch schools for their eighth grade year.

"It wasn't like I had anything to say about it," he says with a wry smile. "It was useless to argue. When my parents decided something, that was it. And they were doing it with the best intentions, I know that. They decided to put me in a big private school in the suburbs, on the other side of the city.

"And *that*," he says firmly, "was where everything went bad."

A DIFFERENT KIND OF SCHOOL

Matt says the main reason he didn't want to change schools was because he didn't want to leave the small, friendly environment he'd always known.

"There were a few kids who would be at the new school," he says, "but they weren't close friends; nobody I really knew well. What I knew about the place scared me a little bit—like that most of the kids were rich kids from the suburbs."

Matt raises a palm to correct himself.

"Actually, there was something I sort of looked forward to about changing schools," he says, grinning. "I wouldn't have to wear a uniform, like I'd been doing for the past seven years. At St. Ann's it had always been brown corduroy pants and a brown shirt. Awful! Really—I'll never wear brown pants again.

"So that was the only positive for me, going in. My mom and dad did tell me that it would be better academically since there would be smaller class sizes, so the teachers would have more time for the kids. It was more structured, too—less fooling around. The plan was that I'd go there for eighth grade and then all the way through high school, too."

A FIRST LOOK

Matt says that the school was expensive, but he was able to work there the summer before he enrolled to offset some of the tuition costs.

"I showed up to do student service, and they got me working right away, cleaning up the school," he says. "I scrubbed floors, cleaned carpets, scraped gum off the walls—you name it. They'd just throw me in a room and tell me what to do. Mostly I worked with the janitors, who were pretty nice guys.

"It wasn't bad, either. Sometimes they'd give me a job that was a little more interesting and the time would go fast. Plus, looking around at the classrooms, I was kind of impressed. I mean, you had to be, coming from a little school like mine. The classrooms were really big, really nice. I remember hoping that I'd do okay as far as grades went, and maybe I'd be able to get into a college."

By the end of the first day of school, however, Matt had changed his mind completely about the school.

"I hated it like I've never hated anyplace else," he says with barely disguised bitterness. "You just don't even know how bad it was. It went sour right away. I walked in, dressed kind of like I'm dressed now, you know? And right off, people are looking at me. Some of them come up and say, 'Hey, where are you from?' like I dropped down from the moon or something."

"I Didn't Even Get It at First"

"I told them I'm from the city, from the north side. And they just made up their minds right then and there about me. Seriously! It is the clickiest school you can imagine. They just snubbed me, like I was some sort of outcast or something. I didn't even get it at first, when they did that.

"Some kids started calling me 'nigger,'" he says disgustedly. "I'm a white kid from the city and because of where I come from and the clothes I'm wearing, they use racist terms like that! I guess they figured, 'Oh, he's from the north side, he must be from a gang, or he does drugs, or whatever.' So they started harassing me, breaking the little combination lock on my locker, ripping up my papers, stealing things. They wrote 'We hate you, nigger' on my stuff."

Matt says that there was a handful of black students at the school, and they were as unfriendly as the others.

"They didn't use the same terms as those other guys," he says. "But they'd do the same stuff. I don't have any idea why. I know that a couple of the kids from my old school that transferred with me had been smart—they told people they were from the parkway, instead of saying 'the north side.' That must have sounded like a rich section of town or something because they didn't get the same treatment."

"That's Life—I Dress Like I Dress"

Matt says he felt picked on because of superficial things, such as the way he dressed.

"At lunchtime we could go outside to eat on nice days. One time I went off school property, heading down to a gas station to get a can of pop. This cop jumps out the second I step off campus. He says, 'Hey, you drug dealing, boy? You better pull those pants up higher,' stuff like that."

Matt shrugs, as if baffled by it all.

"I don't know, I didn't think I was dressed strange at all. It's the way I dress here, where I live. I mean, if they thought *my* pants were low, they should see some of the kids in my neighborhood! I did sort of tone it down after a while—it wasn't like I was trying to get all that attention, you know."

He pauses a moment, thinking.

"But in a way, I really resented the fact that I had to dress a certain way just to get along. I mean, that's life—I dress like I dress. I didn't get all angry with the other students there because they were obsessed with dressing in Polo and Eddie Bauer. It's just a question of taste—nobody's business but my own."

ENDURING THE YEAR

Matt says that one word could sum up how he faced that year: *endure*.

"I basically had no friends," he says. "I sat by myself or with one or two girls I knew from the north side. But mostly I hung out alone. I did find that the only people who were willing to go out on a limb and be friendly were the—I guess you'd call them the freaks, the goths. The ones with pink hair and purple lipstick.

"And then there was this one black girl who came in the middle of the year. She was from the north side, too. We clicked and got to be friends the last part of the year. We just endured together; tried to stay out of everyone else's way."

Matt says that teachers were often no more understanding than the students were.

"Like in the hallways, there was this one senior that really got off nagging me, just egging me on all the time. Every day he was trying to get a fight started. So one day, me and him got in this big fight; I just had enough of him, you know? I was tired of the name calling, him slamming me into the wall when teachers weren't around. So I fought back.

"He was way bigger than me. But all of a sudden this teacher comes out of his classroom and grabs me and starts screaming at me. He tells me I'm going to get suspended! And this senior—the teacher just pats him on the back and sends him back to class. And the kid was like six times bigger than me!"

Matt's urban appearance and attitude made it difficult for him to fit into his new school. "I really resented the fact that I had to dress a certain way just to get along," he complains.

Matt visited the counselor once, hoping to find a sympathetic ear. And while the counselor was not argumentative with him, Matt didn't feel as though he was very understanding.

"I told him what was going on," he explains, "and how everybody is like angry that I'm different from them, and how they think I'm bad because of where I live. Well, his big solution was to put me in this special meeting group at school with kids whose parents are alcoholics and crack users. Great idea, huh?"

"Go There Once"

Was anyone pleasant? Matt thinks hard.

"Yeah, the janitors were nice," he says. "They remembered me from the summer; I did good work for them. And this one art teacher. She was nice to me once I settled down. I admit that I got mad after a while, and I started fighting back. In her class, she had me sitting up in the front by her desk. And kids were throwing stuff at me all the time, just trying to start things. And one time I turned around after someone threw something—I don't even remember what it was—and I got in their face, just started yelling at them. I had to.

"I got in trouble for that and was sent to the principal. He told me to knock it off or I'd get thrown out of 'this fine institution.' Give me a break."

Matt snorts indignantly, remembering.

When asked if the school, the teachers, and the students could really be as bad as he makes them sound, Matt gets a hard look in his eyes.

"Hard to believe?" he asks. "Yeah, well, go there once."

"Like Being Two Different People"

But what about his grades? Did the smaller classes and better teachers have the effect his parents had hoped?

"No, not really," he says. "The work was real hard there. They ability grouped, just like at my old school, and I was in the lower group again. I don't know, it seemed like everything was so unpleasant that the schoolwork was the last priority for me. My grades weren't great because I'd miss class—I'd get into a yelling match with some kid, or I'd walk out because I'd get so mad.

"I know that part was my fault—sometimes I should have just let it roll off my back. But I didn't. And so I'd miss stuff, and then I wouldn't get my homework done because I hadn't heard the teacher explain it. Or I was so mad about things, I didn't listen."

Matt says that one thing never changed: It was a relief to get back home each afternoon.

"It was a little hard, though," he says, "like being two different people. I'd come home and me and my friend Tony would go and play basketball with neighborhood kids, and there was no problem. Everybody was different, everybody was cool with it. But then I'd get up the next day and get in the car with my mom, and she'd drive me to this place where all of that wasn't cool. It was like going to a different planet.

"My dad really tried to help me out," he says. "I joined this intramural basketball league—not like varsity or anything. It was just for fun. My dad came to a game once and jokingly told me, 'Play like you're from the north side.' He thought I should be proud of who I was, and I agreed with him. On the court, I could do that. I mean,

Matt concedes that schoolwork was a low priority for him, and as a result, his grades were poor. "I'd miss class," he admits. "I'd get into a yelling match with some kid, or I'd walk out because I'd get so mad."

I'm short, but I can play street ball. Like some guys would start throwing elbows at me, but I'd jump up with elbows out already. That's easy—you learn to play like that around here. Just plain old street ball. So once in a while I found that I could be myself."

ANOTHER YEAR

By the end of his eighth grade year, Matt had lost a lot of self-confidence. His grades had dropped, and he still felt like an outsider. However, Matt's parents hoped that once he was in the high school section of the school things would improve.

"My parents made me go another year," he says. "They wanted me to give the high school part a chance; they knew it was supposed to be a good school, and they wanted me to do well. But my dad made me a promise: He told me that if I hated it after one more year, he'd let me register at Henry, the public high school in my neighborhood.

"And yeah, I hated it. The first whole week I didn't even go. My parents were sort of distracted, dealing with my older brother at the time—I don't remember exactly why. But I hung out at Tony's every day that first week. They knew I was dragging my heels and I didn't want to go. I'd tell them, too—I didn't lie. I'd say, 'I'm not going today; I just can't handle it now,' and then I'd go stay over at Tony's. His school hadn't started yet.

"I was so jealous of Tony; he was enrolled at Henry, and he wasn't dreading school at all. I knew that's where I wanted to be. Tony tried to help me stay positive. He'd tell me that it would be better this year because I wouldn't be new anymore. He'd remind me that I'd meet more girls and I'd start to fit in better.

"But it was worse, if that was possible. Some of the freaky kids I'd met the year before, the ones who had been civil to me, they'd graduated or left. Usually I didn't have anybody to be with, so I was by myself again. And after school I'd just come home and complain to Tony about how bad my life was.

"THE TEACHERS . . . KIND OF GAVE UP ON ME"

Matt's grades did not improve that year; if anything, they went down.

"I was getting low D's and F's," he says. "I lost my temper more; I'd stick up for myself when I was getting harassed and paid the price. I got in trouble a lot. Plus, the work was harder and harder.

"I don't want to come off sounding like I'm just blaming every-one else, either. I told you before, some of this was my fault. But I didn't start it—that's the truth. But the teachers at that school kind of gave up on me, I think. Like, I'd miss the first half of class be-cause I was down in the principal's office for something. And I'd go on to my class and the teacher would say, 'Well, Matt, you've missed some important stuff here already, so you might as well just stay outside the rest of the hour. You wouldn't understand it anyway.' So I got further and further behind."

Would he have changed his behavior if he could go back and re-live those years at school? Matt shudders and grins.

"What a thought—having to relive that time! I don't think I would have lost my temper the same way, I guess. Instead of get-ting up and swearing when someone did something to me, I could have just sat there maybe."

He thinks hard and shakes his head.

"Really, though, I don't think it would have been right just to sit there and take it," he says. "For instance, we'd be doing a test—an important one, like an achievement test or something—and all of a sudden there'd be a big splash of pop hitting my desk, and the test would be ruined, all soaked. I'd stand up, tell the teacher, and she'd yell at me for having pop in class. I didn't have pop, and I'd tell her that—someone just walked behind me and did it!"

Matt gestures helplessly with his hands.

"I'd get mad, and when I think about it now, I still get mad. The bottom line is that the school and I just weren't a good match."

KEEPING HIS WORD

At the end of his freshman year, Matt's father kept his word. The two of them went to Henry High School to register for Matt's sophomore year, and Matt couldn't have been happier.

"It was such a great feeling that first day of my sophomore year," he remembers. "Just walking in, seeing all the different kids, lots going on. There was so much atmosphere, it seemed so much more real than anything at that other place. And it was so easy to get to know people—after a year, I think I knew almost every kid there!

"And what a change—it was like 80 percent nonwhite at Henry, compared with like four students at the other school. We had Mexi-cans, Asians, blacks, whites, Native Americans. Usually everybody got along fine. Once in a while there'd be a fight outside, when kids who didn't go to the school were around, but not usually.

Matt is grateful for the support of his father, who kept his promise to let Matt enroll in the public high school for his sophomore year. Despite the school change, Matt continued to have trouble with his studies.

"The first few days, I used to sit in class and think about how weird it would be for a kid from that other school to be at Henry— he would have felt about as strange as I did the year before."

PROBLEMS WITH SCHOOLWORK

However, it wasn't long before Matt realized that although the social aspects of Henry were more comfortable, the schoolwork was still difficult for him.

"I don't like reading much," he says, "and I had trouble with it sometimes in school. I'd get bored real fast. I chew gum, I wiggle my feet around, and all of a sudden the page I'm reading seems like a blur for me. Then I'd want to stand up; I didn't want to sit still anymore. It was like—I need to do something else! It was like that in any class where the teacher would tell us to read on our own."

Matt says that some of the teachers suggested that perhaps he had a learning disability and that's why he had trouble.

"That's what they'd say when I'd kind of get out of hand, I guess. They'd say, 'Oh, he's got ADD' (attention deficit disorder) or something, and they'd send me to the learning specialist. My mom would hear this and she'd think, 'Oh, maybe this is the problem he's had all along.'

"But then the specialist would tell me no, that I didn't have ADD. And so the next day I'd go back to class, and then in a little while they'd send me back and say maybe I should be tested for a different learning disability. And the same thing would happen— nothing.

"And really, some of these counselors and specialists would really make me mad. They'd ask me if my parents were on drugs. My *parents*! Or they'd treat me like a criminal—they'd say, 'Oh, is the gang life getting to you?' Or 'Is drug dealing getting hard?' I'd tell them I don't do drugs, and I don't run with any gang. It made me mad, to tell you the truth. And it sort of hurt my feelings, too."

TRYING

Matt remembers how much trouble he had when his English class studied a play by Shakespeare.

"The language in the play was really confusing with all those 'thee's' and 'wherefore's'," he says. "Then we'd watch a movie about it, and I'd really get into it. But then on the test the teacher would ask stuff that wasn't in the movie—it had been just in the play we'd read, and I couldn't do it.

"I did get some help from my journalism teacher, though. He'd show me how it made the words a little easier to visualize if I typed them on a computer, just one at a time. He'd type one, then I'd type it. I just got used to seeing it, spelling it out. It didn't seem so much like a foreign language then.

"Math was hard for me, too—but I think it was just the way the class was set up. See, the teacher had no patience at all—she'd just snap over nothing at all. Like somebody would break the lead on their pencil, and she'd go ballistic. Anyway, she'd give an assignment and give us time to start it in class.

"But she wasn't very good at explaining things, and as soon as she assigned the work everybody would put their hands up, needing her to come over and help them. She'd only get to about half the kids before the bell rang. Then those of us on the half of the room that didn't get help couldn't do the homework. So then the next day she'd work with our half more; but then the other half was behind. It was a bad year for us in math, I think."

AN INSPIRING TEACHER

Matt says that there were some good teachers at school, and his grades did improve somewhat.

"I did better in some things," he says. "I liked my health teacher a lot. He was kind of like me and Tony put together, but older. He was friendly and liked to talk and had a good sense of humor. He could talk to the kids without sounding like a teacher, you know? Like if you had some food in class, he'd say, 'Hey, don't you know you can't have that in here . . . unless you give me some!' So he was okay. We'd do packets of work each day, but after that we'd all sit and just talk to him."

But his favorite class, Matt says with barely concealed pride, was woodshop.

"It was the reason I'd go to school most of the time," he admits, grinning. "I've always been sort of interested in building things. My grandpa was good at carpentry; he died when I was real young, but when we'd go visit my grandma she'd let me tinker with his tools down in the basement. My dad would sit down there with me and explain what each one was for. He had never gotten into it like my grandpa had, but he knew enough to get me started.

"But then I started this class in high school. My teacher was named Mr. Lohn; he was this old army sergeant with a loud voice. I learned so much from him—I can't even begin to tell you how much. And he helped me with math, too. I actually learned more about math from him than from my math teacher, especially about fractions and stuff.

"Mr. Lohn would say, 'Let me teach you the right way to do this, not the Henry way.' He was great—he knew how to explain something so you got it just right. And he knew if you really understood it or whether you were just saying you did to get him off your back. He didn't seem like a teacher, though. If you saw him outside of class, you'd say, man, this guy's a real jerk. He's so hard and mean, with the tone of voice he used.

"My dad really liked him, too. He'd sometimes come in after school and see the projects I was working on, and him and Mr. Lohn would start yacking and they'd get along great, having a great old time."

"IF SCHOOL COULD ALWAYS BE THIS WAY"

In woodshop, Matt found that he was at the top of his class, rather than in a lower ability group.

Matt proudly displays the candleholder he made with the help of his caring woodshop teacher, Mr. Lohn.

"I did really well for him," Matt smiles. "I can show you all the projects I've got in the house that I did in his classes."

He gets up and walks to the living room.

"This candleholder I made," he says, pointing to an attractive piece on the coffee table. "And back in the den, I built this table. And this rocking chair. All of this stuff. The chair was the hardest—but me and him came up with a design, and he showed me what to do, and I did it. It was hard work but very satisfying when it was all done.

"He taught me how to design things myself and really encouraged me to keep at it. He told me I had skill and creativity, which was a real compliment coming from him. Mr. Lohn was willing to explain things to my dad, too—tell him what kinds of tools I'd need for certain projects. The most fun was sometimes if I had an orthodontist appointment, my dad would bring me back to school afterwards. We'd go into Mr. Lohn's room if he didn't have any kids in there at the time. He'd show my dad all the tools, the machines, what each one did. We'd all just sit in there and talk about things. I used to think, boy, if school could always be this way, it'd be great."

"MOST TEACHERS DIDN'T CARE"

It seemed to Matt that, compared to Mr. Lohn, most of his other teachers were disinterested in their students. Some were interested, he says, but they were often too busy trying to control rowdy kids to teach much.

"Most teachers didn't care," he says. "You'd find that out early, especially as a new student. I'd sit there while the teachers would go through their little talk at the beginning of the year, telling what would happen if you broke the rules. And I'd say to myself, okay, we'll see. I'd watch to see what would really happen when a kid did something bad.

"Most of the time, nothing. The teachers would act afraid of the kids, and the kids took advantage of that. In my school it wasn't uncommon at all for kids to take swings at teachers. Walking down the hall, you'd see a teacher run out of her room crying. Then you'd look in to see what was going on, you know? And you'd see a couple of kids taking one of those big teacher desks and flipping it over.

"A lot of the teachers just weren't strict enough. Like some would get up in front of the class and ask the kids if it was okay to study a certain thing. They'd *ask* the kids! Nobody would respect a teacher like that. I think sometimes the problem was that we were overcrowded. In some classes there wouldn't be enough desks; kids would be sitting on the floor in the aisles. There weren't enough books, and that made it hard to teach."

Matt says that some teachers, including Mr. Lohn, were able to handle unruly students.

"My one English teacher—he could keep you in line," he says. "He wore these big steel-toed work boots, and if you fell asleep in class, he'd come over to your desk and wham! He'd kick the desk so hard you'd fall out. And that health teacher I was telling you about? He'd never hit a kid, but if a kid took a swing at him, he'd 'restrain' the kid by kind of picking him up and squeezing him. Man, some of those kids looked like their eyes were popping out!

"Mr. Lohn was pretty good about things—I know he could keep me in line easy. I had him twice a day—once early in the day and then again after lunch. There's no way I could leave after lunch! He was really strict, but you could tell he cared. He didn't need to kick desks or anything like that. He was like a big grandpa. Even if he yelled at me for an hour, I wouldn't care. I'd let him."

"ALL THE TEACHERS JUST GAVE UP"

Unfortunately, Mr. Lohn left at the end of Matt's junior year. By the time he started school as a senior, school without his woodshop teacher seemed to lose most of its appeal, he says.

"I was really sad to see him leave," says Matt. "I gave him my phone number because he'd said that he was going to be building an addition to his house—a big sixty-foot-by-eighty-foot one. I thought maybe I could help him with it, but he never called. Maybe he lost my number, I don't know. I tried calling the school, but they wouldn't give out a teacher's number to a student.

"They replaced Mr. Lohn with a substitute English teacher. This guy didn't even know how to turn on the machines or use any of the tools. We just watched stupid movies like *Scarface* or *Money Talks*. Kids did that, broke windows, jumped out. It was such a waste of time. If Mr. Lohn had been there, he would have hated it, too.

"It seemed like all the teachers just gave up at the same time—not just in woodshop but all the classes. It bothered me because some of the classes were ones that sort of sounded interesting, like science. In my class we made these different structures—you could build any kind of biodome you wanted. Some made aquariums, some made terrariums, whatever. Then we were going to work on them, keep notes of what was happening.

Matt fixes a sandwich in the coffee shop where he works. Although he was eager to leave school, Matt hopes to obtain his GED so he can attend a technical school and learn a trade.

"This was supposed to go on for a month. It sounded kind of cool. But the teacher got bored with it after the second day, and we just stopped doing it. By the third day the teacher had the VCR hooked up, and we were watching videos. Not even science videos, just stupid movies, like in woodshop."

"I REALLY WANTED TO LEAVE"

Matt admits that there aren't many dropouts who wait until part of the way through their senior year to leave.

"I found out in October of that year that there was some trouble with my transcript," he says. "Some of the credits I had from the other school weren't going to count—they were religion credits and Henry didn't accept those. I'd have to make up some classes, too—ones I'd failed.

"I thought about going through the whole year. The way things were going, it seemed like a waste of time. Plus, I didn't look forward to doing summer school and probably another whole year to make up those credits. I really wanted to leave; just get out of there. Tony had already dropped out—the teachers had put him in this program called SPAN (Special Program for Adolescent Needs). He didn't think he should be there because he's not dumb. And he's right, he's not. Anyway, it wasn't like all my friends were at school."

Matt talked to his mother and father about the situation and told them why he wanted to leave.

"My dad was okay about it," Matt says. "He understood, and he knew things weren't the same without woodshop. But he believes in education—he graduated from high school, went into the army, and did college. He told me, 'If you're going to leave one school, you'd better go to another—don't just quit.' But I told him no school was going to be much different. We'd tried public, we'd tried private.

"My mom was sad about the whole thing. I promised I'd take the GED exam and that would work. Mom would rather have me in school, though, and I understand that. But it wouldn't work. I made a promise that I'd get my GED in June, and after that I want to go to some tech school, most likely carpentry."

"I KNOW MYSELF BEST"

Matt currently has a job at a coffee shop, making sandwiches, helping customers, and doing whatever needs to be done. He enjoys the job but knows there are other things he wants to do.

"I give half of every paycheck to my dad," he says. "I'm saving for tech school, so that will be money well spent. I have a girlfriend I spend time with nowadays. She's one of those kids who some people would call a freak. She's got funny hair that sticks out all over and tattoos, and her tongue is pierced. She's a wonderful person; I really like her.

"Hey," he says, "I've got tattoos, too! I've got this one." He takes off his outer shirt, showing a tattoo of a naked lady on one arm and a large blue tattoo on his other—Reservoir Dogs, he explains.

"Wendy, my barber, she asked me why I think I won't regret this later when I'm older. She says, 'Come on, Matt, don't you think you'll regret doing that some day?' I just told her, 'Maybe if I *didn't* get one now, I'd regret it.' I'm planning to get a couple more on my calves. I kind of like the look.

"I think sometimes that the schools really mess up with kids. Like with Tony—it's like they decided he wasn't smart, so they put him in a class with slow kids. And the other kids *were* slow. But he's not. He's really smart; it's just that he doesn't learn the same way as they think he should. He's really good at listening—not much at reading.

"And me, too. I don't know if I've got a learning disability. Probably not. They sure couldn't find one back at Henry. But some teachers just figure if you're not learning at the same rate as everyone else, or in the same way as everyone else, then you're slow. I'm not slow—I know that. I didn't have any trouble learning math with Mr. Lohn, or woodworking, either. I think some people can learn a lot of different ways, from different people. Sometimes, they learn *in spite* of schools."

Epilogue

In the time since these four young people were interviewed for this book, there have been some changes in their lives.

David is now the father of a little girl; however, he and Heather have split up, and his friends are not certain where he is living.

LeAnn's daughter Lanayaiah is six months old and seems to be perpetually teething. LeAnn has decided to register for school this fall and is anxious about her first day.

Matt has put his school plans on hold for a while. He has received a promotion and a raise at the coffee shop where he works, and he isn't as eager to start his vocational school as he was before.

Finally, Alice has dropped out of AA and her treatment program—and has decided that she is able to use alcohol and marijuana "socially" without abusing those drugs. Her mother and father are disappointed, for she had been doing well. However, Alice says she was tired of not doing "normal" things, like attending regular high school, going to the prom, and so on. She has registered at the high school near her house and is hoping to finish her senior year by next summer.

Ways You Can Get Involved

THE FOLLOWING ORGANIZATIONS CAN BE
CONTACTED FOR MORE INFORMATION ABOUT
TEEN DROPOUTS

Cities in Schools
1199 N. Fairfax, Suite 300
Alexandria, VA 22314

This group seeks to aid dropout-prone youths, their families, and
public education throughout the United States.

Migrant Dropout Reconnect Program
BOCES Geneseo Migrant Center
Holcomb Bldg., Room 210
Geneseo, NY 14454

This organization works to decrease the numbers of migrant
farmworker youths who have dropped out of the U.S. public
school system. It also provides placement and children's
services.

National Coalition of Advocates for Students
100 Boylston, Suite 737
Boston, MA 02116

This group unites various organizations with the ideal of pro-
viding educational advocacy to poor, minority, limited English-
proficient, and handicapped youths.

National Dropout Prevention Center (NDPC)
205 Martin St.
Clemson University
Clemson, SC 29634

This organization serves as a clearinghouse of information on school dropout prevention and identifies high-risk youth. In addition, the NDPC provides consultation and referral services to agencies and school systems.

For Further Reading

Nancy Day, *Violence in Schools: Learning in Fear*. Springfield, NJ: Enslow, 1996. Good information on how violence can drive students from school; helpful index.

Debra Goldentyer, *Dropping Out of School*. Austin, TX: Raintree Steck-Vaughn, 1994. Helpful information aimed at students considering dropping out of school.

Jean McBee Knox, *Learning Disabilities*. New York: Chelsea House, 1989. Good index, readable text.

Jeannie Oakes and Martin Lipton, *Making the Best of Schools: A Handbook for Parents, Teachers, and Policymakers*. New Haven, CT: Yale University Press, 1990. Interesting section on the importance of teachers in preventing frustration and failure in students.

Victoria Sherrow, *Dropping Out*. New York: Benchmark Books, 1996. Good section on alternatives to high school.

Index

ABOUT THE AUTHOR

Gail B. Stewart is the author of more than eighty books for children and young adults. She lives in Minneapolis, Minnesota, with her husband, Carl, and their sons, Ted, Elliot, and Flynn. When she is not writing, she spends her time reading, walking, and watching her sons play soccer.

Although she has enjoyed working on each of her books, she says that *The Other America* series has been especially gratifying. "So many of my past books have involved extensive research," she says, "but most of it has been library work—journals, magazines, books. But for these books, the main research has been very human. Spending the day with a little girl who has AIDS, or having lunch in a soup kitchen with a homeless man—these kinds of things give you insight that a library alone just can't match."

Stewart hopes that readers of this series will experience some of the same insights—perhaps even being motivated to use some of the suggestions at the end of each book to become involved with someone of the Other America.

ABOUT THE PHOTOGRAPHER

Carl Franzén is a writer/designer who enjoys using the camera to tell a story. He works out of his home in Minneapolis where he lives with his wife, three boys, two dogs, and one cat. For lots of fun, camaraderie, and meeting interesting people, he coaches youth soccer and edits a neighborhood newsletter.